MW00574672

Workforce Ecosystems

Management on the Cutting Edge series

Abbie Lundberg, editor-in-chief

Published in cooperation with *MIT Sloan Management Review*

The AI Advantage: How to Put the Artificial Intelligence Revolution to Work
Thomas H. Davenport

The Technology Fallacy: How People Are the Real Key to Digital Transformation
Gerald C. Kane, Anh Nguyen Phillips, Jonathan Copulsky, and Garth Andrus

Designed for Digital: How to Architect Your Business for Sustained Success
Jeanne W. Ross, Cynthia Beath, and Martin Mocker

See Sooner, Act Faster: How Vigilant Leaders Thrive in an Era of Digital Turbulence
George S. Day and Paul J. H. Schoemaker

Leading in the Digital World: How to Foster Creativity, Collaboration, and Inclusivity
Amit S. Mukherjee

The Ends Game: How Smart Companies Stop Selling Products and Start Delivering Value
Marco Bertini and Oded Koenigsberg

Open Strategy: Mastering Disruption from Outside the C-Suite
Christian Stadler, Julia Hautz, Kurt Matzler, and Stephan Friedrich von den Eichen

The Transformation Myth: Leading Your Organization through Uncertain Times
Gerald Kane, Rich Nanda, Anh Nguyen Phillips, and Jonathan Copulsky

Winning the Right Game: How to Disrupt, Defend, and Deliver in a Changing World
Ron Adner

The Digital Multinational: Navigating the New Normal in Global Business
Satish Nambisan and Yadong Luo

Work without Jobs: How to Reboot Your Organization's Work Operating System
Ravin Jesuthasan and John W. Boudreau

The Future of Competitive Strategy: Unleashing the Power of Data and Digital Ecosystems
Mohan Subramaniam

Productive Tensions: How Every Leader Can Tackle Innovation's Toughest Trade-offs
Chris B. Bingham and Rory M. McDonald

Working with AI: Real Stories of Human-Machine Collaboration
Thomas H. Davenport and Steven M. Miller

Enterprise Strategy for Blockchain: Lessons in Disruption from Fintech, Supply Chains, and Consumer Industries
Ravi Sarathy

Redesigning Work: How to Transform Your Organization and Make Hybrid Work for Everyone
Lynda Gratton

Inside the Competitor's Mindset: How to Predict Their Next Move and Position Yourself for Success
John Horn

Workforce Ecosystems: Reaching Strategic Goals with People, Partners, and Technologies
Elizabeth J. Altman, David Kiron, Jeff Schwartz, and Robin Jones

Workforce Ecosystems

Reaching Strategic Goals with
People, Partners, and Technologies

Elizabeth J. Altman, David Kiron,
Jeff Schwartz, and Robin Jones

The MIT Press
Cambridge, Massachusetts
London, England

© 2023 Massachusetts Institute of Technology

All rights reserved. No part of this book may be reproduced in any form by any electronic or mechanical means (including photocopying, recording, or information storage and retrieval) without permission in writing from the publisher.

The MIT Press would like to thank the anonymous peer reviewers who provided comments on drafts of this book. The generous work of academic experts is essential for establishing the authority and quality of our publications. We acknowledge with gratitude the contributions of these otherwise uncredited readers.

This book was set in ITC Stone Serif Std and ITC Stone Sans Std by New Best-set Typesetters Ltd. Printed and bound in the United States of America.

Library of Congress Cataloging-in-Publication Data

Names: Altman, Elizabeth J., author. | Kiron, David, author. | Schwartz, Jeff, 1958- author.
Title: Workforce ecosystems : reaching strategic goals with people, partners, and technologies / Elizabeth J. Altman, David Kiron, Jeff Schwartz, Robin Jones.
Description: Cambridge, Massachusetts : The MIT Press, [2023] | Series: Management on the cutting edge | Includes bibliographical references and index. | Summary: "A practical guide for business leaders to manage workers within and outside their organizations"—Provided by publisher.
Identifiers: LCCN 2022026912 (print) | LCCN 2022026913 (ebook) | ISBN 9780262047777 (hardcover) | ISBN 9780262373296 (epub) | ISBN 9780262373302 (pdf)
Subjects: LCSH: Labor supply—Management. | Strategic planning.
Classification: LCC HD5706 .A557 2023 (print) | LCC HD5706 (ebook) | DDC 331.12—dc23/eng/20221125
LC record available at https://lccn.loc.gov/2022026912
LC ebook record available at https://lccn.loc.gov/2022026913

10 9 8 7 6 5 4 3 2 1

Contents

Series Foreword

The world does not lack for management ideas. Thousands of researchers, practitioners, and other experts produce tens of thousands of articles, books, papers, posts, and podcasts each year. But only a scant few promise to truly move the needle on practice, and fewer still dare to reach into the future of what management will become. It is this rare breed of idea—meaningful to practice, grounded in evidence, and *built for the future*—that we seek to present in this series.

—Abbie Lundberg

Editor-in-Chief
MIT Sloan Management Review

Introduction

"How do you define your workforce?"

We have posed this question to dozens of executives and asked it in multiple global management surveys. The most common answer is also the most surprising.

A confident minority of executives say their workforce is just their employees. But the overwhelming majority, especially leaders on the front lines of organizational transformations, include a variety of groups—not just employees—in their workforce definitions.

Since we began our study of the future of the workforce a few years ago, it has become clear that the definition of the workforce is changing. We've talked to executives in many Fortune 500 companies concerning how they think about their workforces. Virtually all acknowledge that long-term contractors, temporary gig workers, professional services firms, subcontractors, app developers, and other complementors play an increasingly significant role in their businesses. Over and over again, we hear different versions of this statement: "Our workforce is made up of those people and groups involved with achieving our business objectives." This broader and more holistic view of who (and what) constitutes a workforce has far-reaching implications.

It implies that the composition and boundaries of the *workforce* have changed. These shifts in workforce semantics portend real-world shifts in management practices. Hierarchical, command-and-control, internally focused management practices are ill-suited for workforces that span internal and external organizational boundaries.

Using siloed functions to independently manage employees and external contributors, for example, is fraught with challenges; ill-defined decision rights, governance processes, and power dynamics can undermine even the most well-intentioned executives. In addition, the technology systems that support the management of employees along with the accessing and tracking of external contributors are typically different and disconnected; their lack of integration creates inefficiencies and inconsistencies that can thwart efforts to obtain and maintain strategically valuable capabilities. Lastly, when a substantial group of workers are not employees, managers have to find ways to lead with less control, which is often an uncomfortable adjustment.

One interview in particular hammered home the significance of intentionally managing both internal and external contributors in an integrated way. An executive of a large global company told us that in March 2020, at the onset of the COVID-19 pandemic, "We began figuring out how to handle things like pay continuity, absenteeism, and the need for leaves of absence for those employees who couldn't work remotely, such as our teammates in distribution centers and company-owned production facilities. But we quickly realized we needed to consider our contingent workforce as well. That was the initial impetus that really drove us to say, 'OK, so how big is that box? Do we know who and where they are? Can we find them quickly if we need to?' And when we say we want to do the right thing for our extended family of workers, are we all defining that family the same way?"

We see similar examples across the business landscape: companies recognizing, belatedly, their dependence on a wide range of contributors and then taking seriously the need to manage their complex, interconnected workforces in a more intentional way. As more than one executive told us, "We woke up one day to find that 30 to 50 percent of our workforce consists of workers who are not employees."[1] Some became acutely aware of their situation because of the pandemic. Others had already recognized that the nature of their workforce had changed.

External contributors and partners of various types have become much more than stopgaps, low-wage doers, or temporary fill-ins; they have become essential to many companies' business successes. The availability of high-end contingent workers is expanding rapidly, as are companies' new abilities to find, engage, and continuously manage them. In some industries—like energy and information technology (IT)—it is not uncommon for a business's external contributors to outnumber its employees. As one exasperated executive asked, "Wouldn't it make sense to become just as mature about managing external contributors, a segment that can be even bigger than your payroll workers?"

This trend toward more external contributors goes beyond gig workers. The digital economy has created new possibilities for one company to add value to another company's products. Manufacturers of online games, cell phones, and automobiles, for instance, increasingly depend on app developers (and thus app availability) for the success of their products. The existence of these so-called complementors is not new, but their importance to companies has grown over time. They help deliver valuable outcomes without traditional statements of work, or tax forms like W-2s or 1099s in the United States. They do work for the enterprise, but are seldom managed by those responsible for employees, such as human resources (HR). Executives are beginning to ask whether they should continue to manage complementors separately from other workers and contributors to value creation.

As companies wean themselves from an employee-centric approach to their workforce, they are often forced to experiment with new management techniques. They have no best practices to draw from; there are no precedents, guideposts, or playbooks. Leaders need a useful framework for leading as well as managing internal and external contributors in a more integrated way.

This book provides that framework, which our research indicates must address four basic questions:

1. What management practices are necessary to access, develop, and engage both internal and external contributors over time?
2. How do organizations' functional relationships need to change to achieve valuable business outcomes with many types of work contributors?

3. How do leadership mindsets and behaviors need to change to effectively and fairly manage an interdependent group of internal and external contributors?

4. What technology systems and data are necessary to effectively access and engage both internal and external contributors?

These questions penetrate to the foundations of business. Addressing them requires an entirely new approach, not an incremental response. We contend that this new approach should be based on workforce ecosystems.

Toward Workforce Ecosystems

Before explaining in more detail what workforce ecosystems are and how to orchestrate them, we want to offer some reasons for using the term *workforce ecosystem.*

Ecosystem implies complex, interdependent parts functioning together. Engaging many types of workers and other contributors creates interdependencies among multiple actors; each may have their own separate goals, but the firm relies on all participants to come together to get work done. What's more, ecosystems have been a useful metaphor for describing relationships between business entities for decades. Within management and academic circles, authors have used ecosystem structures to represent systems that are highly interconnected and interdependent. They showcase complementarities where participants may not be contractually linked, but create products that work together and share common customers. While ecosystem analogies have been widely used to represent connections between organizations, they have yet to be extensively applied to encompass relationships between organizations as well as between the people working within and with them.

In the business arena, a growing number of organizations describe their workforces as ecosystems. Executives at some organizations, including IBM and NASA, explicitly portray their workforces as ecosystems. Others discuss new organizational behaviors that sound a lot like managing a workforce ecosystem. We also discovered organizations that had intentionally established a workforce ecosystem at the core of their business model. In part I, we describe one such company. With only four hundred employees, its workforce ecosystem includes over one million contributors around the globe.

Many of the executives we interviewed were explicitly concerned about providing good jobs, reducing exploitation, and improving diversity, equity, and inclusion (DE&I). Those organizations that embraced an expansive view of the workforce frequently had an equally expansive view of their social responsibilities. With today's heightened concern for workers, we believe that workforce ecosystems can explain, and help leaders more effectively manage, a wide range of dynamics in highly complex and interconnected workforces along with the organizations they serve.

Thus the terminology of workforce ecosystems is apt for several reasons. It resonates with executives; some are already using the language of ecosystems to depict their workforces. Applying the ecosystem concept to workforces is a natural extension of existing research on business ecosystems. Finally, the ecosystem concept enables useful discussions about how to understand and meet responsibilities to a wide range of workers, contributors, and other stakeholders in and beyond the organization.

So what is a workforce ecosystem? We define it this way:

A workforce ecosystem is a structure that encompasses actors, from within the organization and beyond, working to create value for an organization. Within the ecosystem, actors work toward individual and collective goals with interdependencies and complementarities among the participants.[2]

The emphasis on structure comes directly from the ecosystem academic research literature. All ecosystems are structures. That doesn't mean they are rigid. As with biological systems, workforce ecosystem structures can be dynamic: actors come and go, goals change, and relationships shift.

While workforce ecosystems are gaining traction in the business landscape, leaders are not yet intentionally managing their organizations and relationships with external contributors as if they were operating in a highly interconnected ecosystem context. We see pockets of management practices shifting, but by and large, companies are not yet managing their workforce ecosystems any differently than they would a traditional employee-centric hierarchical organization.[3] Similarly, we observe that leaders rarely factor workforce ecosystem thinking into broader business strategy formulation and decision-making.

Exceptions exist. We interviewed executives who recognize that this lack of focus on external contributors is an urgent challenge to their strategy and operations. Their stories and insights inform much of our thinking around how to orchestrate workforce ecosystems.

Because workforce ecosystems are a nascent phenomenon with few best practices, each chapter includes a set of "action questions" that leaders should ask themselves (and in some cases, their teams) as their organizations advance in building and orchestrating workforce ecosystems. It is too soon to say which practices are best; for now, as leaders shift to managing workforce ecosystems, the best practice is to ask the right questions.

Why Workforce Ecosystems Matter Today: Trends Driving Emergence and Growth

The emergence of workforce ecosystems is new, but they are a natural product of several long-standing trends: the decreasing costs of information, the changing nature of work, worker preference shifts, and advances in technology.

Reduced Information Costs

Yochai Benkler, professor at Harvard Law School and faculty codirector of the Berkman Klein Center for Internet and Society, has written extensively on how society is becoming more network-based with decentralized structures. In his 2006 book, *The Wealth of Networks*, Benkler contrasted the industrial economy, in which production was generally constrained by physical requirements (one couldn't easily produce a steam engine in one's home office), with the networked information economy, in which individuals around the world have access to equipment necessary to contribute to production through their computers and network connections. Most important for our discussion, he highlights how the ability to produce value without needing resources from a central organization has led to new models of production and hence new models of organizing. He explains,

> The high capital costs that were a prerequisite to gathering, working, and communicating information, knowledge, and culture, have now been widely distributed in the society. The entry barrier they posed no longer offers a condensation point for the large organizations that once dominated the information environment. Instead, emerging models of information and cultural production, radically decentralized and based on emergent patterns of cooperation and sharing, but also of simple coordinate coexistence, are beginning to take on an ever-larger role in how we produce meaning—information, knowledge, and culture—in the networked information economy.[4]

Workforce ecosystems are an outgrowth of these trends and reflect evolving organizational practices. With individuals able to accomplish work from anywhere, without need for physical access to resources, not only can they work as remote employees, but they can more easily serve as individual contractors. Workers can span organizations, doing work for more than one entity at a time. For example, a gig worker might be engaged by several companies at once, or a person primarily employed by one company might also work one or two side jobs. The upshot is that organizations have more flexibility in how they can address workforce needs and workers have more choices.

Rather than concentrating on hiring particular workers and creating hierarchical structures to organize them, enterprises can embrace a more outcome-centered approach. Dave Ulrich, Rensis Likert collegiate professor of business administration and director of the Human Resources Executive Program at the University of Michigan's Stephen M. Ross School of Business, believes that "the definition of organization is morphing." Indeed, in a workforce ecosystem, networks replace silos and hierarchies. If organizations are no longer characterized by employees in jobs arranged into functional and product-based hierarchies, how then should organizations be defined? For Ulrich, the organization has evolved from a hierarchy to an ecosystem that he imagines as a hub with spokes. In an ecosystem, he says, "the parts are connected through shared capabilities."

The Changing Nature of Work

Historically, when we consider *work*, we think of processes along with a focus on consistency and efficiency. For centuries, standard operating procedures (SOPs) have dominated the landscape for those who study work processes. Today, from factory floors to software development, we see a shift to project-based work and an emphasis on outcomes. For example, Meredith Wellard, Deutsche Post DHL Group's vice president of group learning, talent, and platforms, notes that a much higher percentage of the courier company's work is now project based. "As an organization, we're focused on being the best at delivering what the customer or the colleague needs to be successful," she says. "And you can only do that with the agile way of working, with constant project-like work."

Jennifer Felch, Chief Digital Officer and CIO of Dell Technologies, affirms that the technology company, partly in response to the shift to remote work, is embracing work that is project based and directed at outcomes. "In a more virtual world, you have to measure the results that people produce, not the time they're putting in at the office," she explains. "I think that's really well suited for today's worker who is motivated by purpose-driven work that makes a difference." Felch goes on to say, "This requires us to attract and retain talent of all kinds, including full-time and contract, while also providing an environment that enables flexibility and work-life balance." This shift to a dynamic, frequently shifting blend of workers changes how one conceives of structures that have traditionally been more static and enduring.

The transition to project-based arrangements appeals to both younger and older workers, says Arun Srinivasan, operating partner at Banyan Software, a holding company for enterprise software businesses. "Workers who are just joining the workforce and those who are toward the last segment of their careers are both expressing a desire to engage in a different way," he observes. "They're saying, 'I want to do meaningful work. I want purpose behind that work, however I choose to engage under these circumstances.'" Workforce ecosystems lend themselves to an approach characterized by various types of workers engaged via different paths, with their own goals and aspirations, moving in and out of an ecosystem structure.

This new model undermines traditional management systems anchored by job descriptions. Semiannual reviews as well as merit increases are predicated on employees remaining in jobs for extended periods and generally pursuing prescribed, linear career paths. Researchers worldwide are seeing a shift toward more short-term, skills-focused, team-based work engagements in which automation and technology free up people's capacity.[5]

Additionally, researchers are highlighting the reemergence of "craft approaches to work" that include not only an emphasis on skills but also the importance of *attitudes* that relate to a devotion to work and concern for impacts on communities.[6] This trend stresses more human-centric perspectives, incorporating concerns related to value and meaning beyond the traditional focus on efficiencies and cost, and illustrates the continued evolution of mindsets that develop in tandem with technologies.

Organizations are focusing more comprehensively on customer offerings that demand extensive collaboration. Alan Trefler, founder and CEO of cloud-based software company Pegasystems, explains the transformation in his own business: "We have been accelerating our involvement with partners who offer complementary elements to what we deliver, and that, I think, is going to become an increasingly large part of our business." This reflects a move to a workforce ecosystem model that incorporates external collaborators in value creation activities.

In a similar spirit, Jared Mueller, director of the Mayo Clinic Innovation Exchange, describes an innovation driven by the famed medical center headquartered in Rochester, Minnesota. The feat was accomplished by a multidisciplinary team in response to a pressing problem:

the transmission of COVID-19 during medical procedures. He says that a "seamless collaboration" among a far-flung team of physicians, engineers, and business strategists led to the creation of a tool to decrease such transmission. Mueller credits "the rapidity with which people across the country, within Mayo and outside of Mayo, fluidly working as one team, were able to get connected with an S&P 500 company, which Mayo has worked with in the past, to create a product that could be broadly distributed, and which is currently in use." This highlights how an organization can orchestrate a workforce ecosystem as it pulls together contributors from disparate independent organizations and locations.

As businesses grapple with more complex interdisciplinary problems, they are searching for innovative solutions that cross domain boundaries. To address these cross-functional challenges, enterprises are relying on blended teams, open innovation, collective intelligence efforts, and other ways of organizing beyond functional and organizational boundaries. Individuals skilled in subjects outside a particular area may bring new sets of eyes and provide novel solutions. These people may reside within an organization or be out in the broader community, such as those engaged through crowdsourcing, innovation challenges, and related models.

In addition to approaches that engage external workers, organizations are bringing together internal employees to tackle problems outside their usual domains. At Dell, internal hackathons invite a cross-functional approach to problem-solving. "The culture of big companies can get siloed," Felch observes. "Welcome to the hackathon—now you can propose ideas about other people's areas. And usually you're on the hook to help deliver it, so that builds bridges across the organization." This creates a workforce ecosystem structure within an organization, even if the interactions are transient.

To cite an example of a function becoming more interdisciplinary, Jacqui Canney, chief people officer at ServiceNow, notes that marketing roles now involve "data science, digital, and e-commerce, juxtaposed against the traditional ways of marketing."

Worker Perspectives on Workforce Ecosystems

Entire books have been written, and are surely being written now, on changes in worker perspectives, especially post-2020. Even before the global pandemic forced moves to remote working, people were approaching the work portion of their lives in dramatically new ways. Individuals were demanding increased flexibility and choice, particularly around location, purpose, and shifts related to life stages. These trends continue to evolve. Workers expect increasing autonomy in what they work on, and in how, where, and when they work. We see a desire to be part of open and inclusive organizations, with pay that is fair (at rates regularly tuned to the market) and aligned with outcomes. Workers are seeking project-based work with frequent opportunities to join and leave projects (referred to as *on-ramping* and *off-ramping*), and searching for opportunities to acquire new skills and experiences from employers as well as via other means (such as traditional education, online options, and credentialing) to increase their value in targeted ways. They are also wary of exploitation and concerned about what can go wrong, especially in compensation and benefits, but also with regard to harassment and discrimination. All of these worker perspectives can vary depending on geography, age, and other demographic categories.

Technology Shifts

Technology is affecting workforce ecosystems in multiple ways, with prominent roles in shaping, supporting, and participating in workforce ecosystems. These roles encompass five different categories: *work technologies*, the tools that workers use to help them do their jobs (e.g., medical diagnostic tools); *workforce technologies*, such as internal workforce management systems and external labor platforms; *workplace technologies* that enable workers to work from anywhere, such as video collaboration tools; *credentialization and verification technologies* that allow workers to manage credentials and employers to verify them, and that increasingly involve blockchain and related technologies; and *technology as participant in workforce ecosystems*, encompassing technologies that participate in the workforce, like software bots (software programs that perform such tasks as interacting with customers through online chat functionality) and automation robots.

Increasingly, organizations have access to these technologies and tools, allowing them to more efficiently deploy resources to reach their strategic goals. Sophisticated matching algorithms used by platform-based businesses enable organizations to find external workers to accomplish tasks that previously would have been performed by internal employees. Blockchain technologies and nonfungible tokens (NFTs, or data units that can't be interchanged) are beginning to enable hiring organizations to verify credentials of workers and keep these verifications updated as employees continue to gain credentials. We explore these trends in more detail in chapter 7. For now, suffice it to say that we are seeing more organizations embracing workforce ecosystems in part because they have growing access to tools that enable their operation.

About the Research

MIT Sloan Management Review and Deloitte Consulting launched a multiyear research project a few years ago to explore the future of the workforce. The authors of *Workforce Ecosystems* have been the principal researchers on that work, which is part of the *MIT Sloan Management Review*'s Big Ideas Initiatives and the genesis for this book. Together with our colleagues, we set out to combine discussions with thought leaders around the world with extensive survey techniques to determine what trends are affecting workforces today and how we can envision workforces evolving into the future. We talked with big and small companies, nonprofit organizations, military establishments, venture investors, international executives, and others. The primary data collection occurred between 2019 and 2022. Appendix B outlines the research process for each year.

Our interviewees were incredibly generous with their time, and forthcoming with their insights and ideas, as they discussed challenges and opportunities with us. The project opened our eyes to a new way in which leaders and organizations are transforming how they approach organizing and managing resources to accomplish strategic goals. Aligned with conversations about how organizations themselves are changing, we have recognized that individuals are reevaluating how, where, when, and in what ways they desire to participate in the labor force worldwide. Through our data collection and analyses, including formal and informal conversations, we have created a framework for how to think about today's, and arguably tomorrow's, workforce. As the title of this book reflects, we have started to think about workforces in terms of *workforce ecosystems*.

A Map of the Book

Organizations are expanding their reach by engaging with a range of contributors to help them achieve strategic goals. In the following chapters, we address how this relates to strategy, leadership and organizational culture, technology enablers, management practices, ethics, and societal implications. In many instances, we draw on case studies and interviews to provide illustrations and share a variety of perspectives.

This book is divided into three parts. The first one explains what workforce ecosystems are. The second part discusses how to manage or orchestrate them. The third part looks at the ethical and societal implications of workforce ecosystems. We conclude with some predictions about the future of workforce ecosystems.

Part I: Introducing Workforce Ecosystems
In part I, we introduce the concept of workforce ecosystems and how they influence strategy.

Chapter 1: Addressing an Extended Workforce   We discuss case examples from three very different organizations: Novartis, Applause, and Walmart. We also explore how other organizations are using analogies to reconceptualize their workforces.

Chapter 2: What Is a Workforce Ecosystem?   In this chapter, we delve deeply into our definition of workforce ecosystems. We explain why each part of the definition is important, and why understanding the definition helps leaders manage these wide-reaching structures.

Chapter 3: Strategy and Workforce Ecosystems   Workforce ecosystems allow leaders and managers to think differently about how they develop, and execute toward, strategic goals and objectives. In this chapter, we provide a perspective on developing strategy that incorporates workforce ecosystems. We present characteristics of workforce ecosystems— the Three Cs of comprehensiveness, community, and coordination —which allow us to distinguish between different kinds of workforce ecosystems and incorporate them into strategic discussions.

Part II: Orchestrating Workforce Ecosystems
Workforce ecosystems require a dramatic shift in how leaders manage a portfolio of contributors. This section provides a comprehensive view of *orchestrating* workforce ecosystems encompassing leadership and management challenges as well as discussing the multiple roles of technologies.

Chapter 4: A Framework for Workforce Ecosystem Orchestration   We present a framework for orchestrating workforce ecosystems that highlights four key themes and takes a cross-functional perspective. In this chapter, we offer a brief introduction to the framework and quick summaries of the themes that we address in the coming chapters.

Chapter 5: Leadership Approaches in Workforce Ecosystems   Here we emphasize key topics related to leadership approaches in workforce ecosystems. We look at the need to relinquish control, lead across organizational boundaries, address board-level topics, and examine implications for organizational culture.

Chapter 6: Integration Architectures for Workforce Ecosystems   Workforce ecosystems include interdependencies and complementarities, which describe relationships between ecosystem participants. In this chapter we discuss integration architectures or how leaders can approach managing these relationships. We focus on relationships within an organization, such as cross-functional collaboration, and also with external contributors.

Chapter 7: Technology Enablers   This chapter considers the multiple roles that technologies play in shaping, supporting, and participating in workforce ecosystems. We present five roles that technologies fill in workforce ecosystems: work tech, workforce tech, workplace tech, credentialization and verification tech, and technology as a participant in workforce ecosystems. We describe each of these and explain how they impact workforce ecosystems.

Chapter 8: Accessing Workforce Ecosystem Members   One of the defining features of workforce ecosystems is that they include an extended workforce incorporating internal and external contributors, such as employees, long-term contractors, gig workers, professional service providers, subcontractors, complementors, and others. Traditional recruiting models no longer suffice to address today's workforce ecosystem needs. In this chapter focusing on management practices, we examine new ways to attract workforce ecosystem participants. We look at the shift to more skills-focused access, and discuss digital labor markets and platforms.

Chapter 9: Aligning Interests with Workforce Ecosystems   This chapter builds on the topics in chapter 8 with a detailed exploration of management practice shifts for workforce ecosystems. We discuss learning and development, career planning, coaching performance, and aligning interests with workforce ecosystem participants.

Part III: Developing Socially Responsible Workforce Ecosystems
The broad adoption of workforce ecosystems leads to ethical considerations within organizations and in society at large. This section explores both internal ethical topics and the implications of the broad-based adoption of workforce ecosystems on society; it also weighs how policy decisions and other macro factors are likely to influence as well as be influenced by workforce ecosystems.

Chapter 10: Ethics in Workforce Ecosystems   Moving from an employee-based view of the workforce to a workforce ecosystem has ethical implications. This chapter revolves around several ethical challenges in workforce ecosystems; these include advancing DE&I for employees and other workers, the ethical treatment of labor platform users who may not be classified as employees, and the responsibilities for third-party workers.

Chapter 11: Implications for Social Responsibility   This chapter addresses how workforce ecosystems are affecting public policy and social safety nets. Among other topics, it looks at corporate responsibility for economic security and good jobs.

Chapter 12: Perspectives on the Future of Workforce Ecosystems   This section considers how workforce ecosystems may evolve and affect the future of the workforce. It discusses the potential emergence of new management practices and speculates on what workforce ecosystems could mean from the perspective of various actors, including individuals, businesses, and society.

I Introducing Workforce Ecosystems

1   Addressing an Extended Workforce

Depending on external contributors to perform work is not a new phenomenon. What has changed? A growing number of companies are discovering that they have crossed a threshold. Their reliance on an extended workforce—including not only employees but also long-term contractors, gig workers, professional service providers, subcontractors, complementors, and even technologies—has become so essential to their business, brand, and approach to value creation that they need to think differently about, and act differently toward, their entire workforce.[1] We see this shift happening in organizations large and small, across a variety of industries. Leaders are redefining who and what constitutes their workforce, and experimenting with, searching for, and creating new management practices.

To start, we share three cases from Novartis, Applause, and Walmart. These three companies are in different industries, operate in different regulatory environments, and have different revenue levels. Yet their stories share a common core. They reflect an expansive view of the workforce and an ongoing search for a more integrated approach to orchestrating a wide range of value creators. Their stories illustrate what companies may encounter as they adopt and embrace workforce ecosystems.

Novartis

Our workforce is anyone who contributes to executing work toward our purpose and business strategy.
—Markus Graf, Novartis

Graf, born in Germany, is currently vice president of HR and global head of talent at Novartis, the Swiss pharmaceutical giant. Before joining Novartis in 2020, Graf was PepsiCo's head of talent management and organization development for Europe and sub-Saharan Africa, a region with approximately 50,000 employees across sixty developed and emerging countries. Before joining PepsiCo, Graf worked for fifteen years in the pharmaceutical industry for Boehringer Ingelheim and Merck. Throughout his career, Graf's roles have spanned HR, IT, project management, and business leadership, and he has worked at the country, regional, and global levels. He is a sought-after speaker globally as a thought leader on new ways of organizing work.

Graf has an expansive view of Novartis's workforce. It includes, he says, "internal people who are on our payroll . . . and we talk right now about 110,000 people at Novartis on our own payroll. We also specifically look at the roughly 50,000 external people that are in our systems."

He believes the external workforce will continue to increase at a rate of 2 percent per year for the foreseeable future; by contrast, he expects the numbers of internal employees to either hold steady or decrease. In the last twelve to eighteen months, notes Graf, Novartis has increased its emphasis on managing the entire workforce. He adds, "We will continue to focus more on managing the external workforce, our total workforce, more intentionally."

Graf offers several reasons for the growth in the external workforce. Novartis is looking for external help to complete work, access skills lacking among its employee base, and create flexibility. "It's becoming even more important in areas where skilled talent is less inclined to join a traditional workforce, such as data scientists and other data workers," he explains. "We see huge opportunities to tap into this external workforce."

Like many other companies, Novartis engages external workers to perform lower- and higher-value work, and in high volumes. Companies like Novartis are able to access highly skilled workers through online platforms such as Toptal as well as via partnerships with staffing agencies that increasingly work with specialized workers such as software engineers and scientists. Nearly a third of Novartis's workforce are external, contingent workers. Novartis is a prime example of a firm rapidly changing how it conceives of and manages its workforce.

Given its dependence on external workers, Novartis is aiming to develop a cross-functional approach that will inform workforce strategies. This effort has already led to new relationships. The procurement function, for example, was often responsible for obtaining external contingent workers. But as external contributors became increasingly significant to Novartis's strategic workforce and efforts to become more agile and flexible, Graf recalls that led to a change:

> We set up steering committees to really bring together these units (procurement and human resources) that should have been interrelated, but have not been interrelated fully. We're also working toward what we call a "talent skills ecosystem" because we recognize at the end of the day, it's about skills and getting access to specific skills, and really building up a common taxonomy, common language, of how do we categorize and codify specific skills.

Data is a major impediment to building a skills taxonomy for Novartis's entire workforce. Graf says the company has good data on only 20 percent of its external contributors. "The number one challenge for us is getting proper data on external workers," he acknowledges. "There's a lot we need to learn about this group." In essence, the challenge is that companies can access résumés and potentially performance rankings on external platforms, but they can't yet obtain skills data that is as granular as they might have for their own employees. Also, systems compatibility remains an issue, so even if detailed data did exist in some form on an external platform, it might not port easily into a company's internal systems. Thus learning about external contributors requires investment and new processes to collect, sort, and integrate data on their skills, interests, and experience.

Even with a skills taxonomy, Graf recognizes that his team needs to work closely with hiring managers to kick the habit of posting a job whenever they need someone. "That's the barrier that I want to break," he says. "You want to help them to understand their different pools of talent and recommend to them suitable options: in terms of costs, but also speed, capability, or skills level so that they can identify the right mix."

Novartis recognizes and is actively managing the changing nature of its workforce. The company is beginning to cross-functionally orchestrate its workforce, with new organizational architectures, management practices, and technology systems. It acknowledges that operational managers need new tools and behaviors to operate within this ecosystem. Leaders are redefining their roles and responsibilities as well.

Applause

Applause provides software testing services. But we don't employ a single tester. . . . You know why? Because we use our community to test our software. That's rule number one.

—Doron Reuveni, Applause

Born and raised in Israel, Reuveni, executive chairman of the board and former CEO of software testing company Applause, started his career in the Israeli army. As a member of the elite Unit 8200 intelligence corps, he attended Technion, the Israel Institute of Technology, to study computer science. Reuveni later moved into managing large research and development as well as engineering teams, and eventually became a market-focused business manager. Opportunity brought him to Boston, where he worked through the internet bubble and crash of the late 1990s and early 2000s, after which he returned to Israel. In 2007, along with a cofounder, Reuveni began exploring software testing and software quality. They recognized that regardless of how much money firms were spending on testing, quality, tools, and applications, users often had trouble using software. Different device configurations, browser fragmentation, localized versions, and so forth led to buggy and unreliable software.

At the time, online communities were a relatively new phenomenon. Facebook, launched in 2004, didn't open to noncollege students until 2006. LinkedIn, which currently boasts eight hundred million members, had only nine million users in January 2007, but was growing at a rate of a hundred thousand members per week.[2] Reuveni and his partner recognized that people were increasingly connecting via online communities, and they saw the value of harnessing online digital communities to perform work.

Reuveni moved back to Boston and successfully raised funding to get Applause off the ground. Eventually, the company grew from a desktop and web-based system to one that tests software on more than 2.5 million devices, including cars, fitness trackers, enterprise applications, and more. A growing, nimble company, Applause manages a large-scale business due primarily to its ability to harness an enormous, crowdsourced community through its uTest subsidiary. The company employs roughly four hundred people, but its community of testers is over one million people strong and growing by more than ten thousand new testers per month.[3] The Applause tester community is the largest in the world. The company pays millions of dollars monthly to its community of testers composed of individuals working on distinct test projects.

At any given time, about 25 to 30 percent of the testers, called uTesters, work on revenue-generating projects for Applause. The rest participate in the Applause software testing community by taking courses on testing, participating in webinars, or contributing content to the community. Anyone can join the community and take classes, says Reuveni. Membership does not depend on how one chooses to participate. Testers can choose assignments (based on interest and the pay offered) or decline them. As Reuveni explains, "They don't have to do anything, they don't have a boss," and elaborates, "Culturally we treat them like they're employees. No difference. Technically, from a legal perspective, they're different."

Reuveni notes that data plays a critical role in validating testers' competencies: "It's much better than hiring someone to do a job because when you hire someone you look at their résumé and you check references. Here, you actually have data of what that person did in the last three years, which projects did they work on, what grading, which bugs did they submit or whatever. You have real data on their value." With that data, Applause can identify and invite specific uTesters to participate on a project. The testers, in turn, can choose to participate or not.

He describes uTesters as a community. They share a name. They are affiliated with a brand (Applause). They have a shared affinity around software testing and software quality. And uTesters have access to a uTest university. The community, Reuveni says, "is really an ecosystem" that cuts across demographics, geographies, and cultures.

> If you look at demographics within our community, the ratio between women and men is 42 percent women and 58 percent men. . . . It's so much better than what you would get in regular high tech. Why? Because we provide for different types of diversity. You can work from home. You can work on your own time. You can have a day job. You can have a life, right? The diversity is much stronger. Plus, because we have so many different cultures within the community and within the employee base, there's a much better understanding of the needs and behaviors of different cultures than I've seen before.

Given this structure, it is not surprising that Reuveni, like Novartis's Graf, has an expansive view of the workforce. He remarks,

> When I think about the workforce, I think about everyone that basically works for a company in order to get things done. From my perspective that includes a broad range, starting with employees to different types of vendors and service providers. Maybe the old traditional offshore, onshore model in certain types of markets. Expanding to communities and crowdsourcing, and even expanding to different types of betas and feedback around separate communities that you create for your products or your brand. I truly think about workforce in a big holistic way.

In sum, the Applause business model, retaining a smaller central organization while building and managing an extensive digital community, offers an extreme case of an effective workforce ecosystem. By integrating internal and external contributors, Applause can provide services well beyond those that would be customary for an organization of its size; its workforce ecosystem, to borrow a boxing metaphor, allows it to punch well above its weight.

Walmart

> I believe the workforce is the composition of all the people who contribute to the strategy or the business objectives of an organization.
> —Donna Morris, Walmart

Morris is the executive vice president and chief people officer at Walmart Inc. in Bentonville, Arkansas. Walmart is the world's largest company by revenue ($559 billion in fiscal year end 2021).[4] Morris is a member of the executive committee and responsible for all company talent-related activities. Before joining Walmart in February 2020, she spent almost eighteen years at Adobe, where she led the HR function and was responsible for the employee experience organization, which included not only customary HR responsibilities but also real estate and security operations for over 20,000 employees across more than seventy-five locations worldwide. Morris has served on the board of directors of the Society for Human Resource Management (SHRM), with over 300,000 members globally. In short, she is a seasoned executive who has operated at the highest levels of the HR profession.

Like Graf and Reuveni, Morris has an expansive view of her company's workforce, which includes Walmart's 2.2 million employees worldwide (almost 1.6 million in the United States) and many other external contributors as well.[5] In her view, everyone who contributes to Walmart's strategic goals is part of its workforce. She explains,

> When I say all the people, they could be directly employed or they could be indirectly employed. Those are two big buckets. When I say indirectly employed, that could mean individuals employed by a third party that you have a relationship with or temporaries who may not be on your payroll. They could be directly employed by you. But at the end of the day, it's all the people who are contributing to driving your business outcomes.

External contributors are playing a larger role in Walmart's workforce, in part because of advances in technology. Platforms enable Walmart to manage flexible workforces *at scale* in an efficient way (e.g., with sophisticated scheduling) that wasn't possible in the past. "You can use a platform to engage services for the needs that you have, whether those are very transitional in nature or longer term," Morris says.

In the future, Morris anticipates that Walmart will use digital platforms to collect a community of workers near a store to help with fulfillment and distribution. She notes that freelancers and contractors will play a more prominent role in Walmart's workforce, and individuals will have increasing control over where and when they work. As she puts it, people will be "the agents of their own opportunity."

The growth in external contributors has implications for how leaders think about inclusion. "Leadership is something we should all be acutely quizzical about in terms of the future of the workforce," Morris asserts, adding,

> Wherever you get your workforce, you need to determine how to best engage the strengths and capabilities of as many people who want to be engaged in the workforce as possible. If you're really going to drive creativity and innovation, you have to engage people across the diversity spectrum. . . . Leaders have to bear in mind all the opportunity to unlock the human potential of people who want to contribute in some fashion.

Novartis, Applause, and Walmart are in different industries, at different scales, and operate in different regulatory environments. Yet all three companies find themselves considering ways to manage a workforce that extends across internal and external organizational boundaries. Their approach to workforce management goes far beyond the HR function, touching leadership, organizational behaviors, technology and data systems, and a wide range of management practices. Their efforts reflect a central theme of this book: many companies are embracing the complexity of their workforce and adopting a more proactive, intentional approach to orchestrating their entire workforce, not just their employees.

| Software
Bots | Complementors | Service
Providers | Freelancers/
Gig Workers | Long-Term
Contractors | Part-/Full-Time
Employees |

Figure 1.1
Workforce continuum conceptualization.

Workforce Analogies

Our interviews revealed that executives embracing a complex, interconnected workforce have different ways of conceptualizing their workforce structures. Their compelling analogies offer insights into how
they interpret the composition and boundaries of their workforces. As
a group, these analogies, described below, point to the need for a more
robust framework that accounts for the dynamic relationships among
a range of workforce participants. As we'll discuss in the next chapter,
workforce ecosystems fill this need.

Workforce as a Continuum

A number of experts consider their workforce to be a continuum that
spans multiple types of contributors. When asked how she defines
a workforce, Barbry McGann, managing director and senior vice
president at Workday Ventures, explains, "We think of it as a continuum of workers from contingent, freelancers, hourly workers to
salary workers."

While Nicholas Skytland, chief of the exploration technology office
at NASA Johnson Space Center, works in a different type of organization, an independent agency of the US government, his workforce definition is strikingly similar. "I define the workforce as a continuum," he
says. "On one end is a human full-time employee and the other end is a
bot." (Many organizations are beginning to consider technologies to be
members of their workforce, as we'll explore later.) Figure 1.1 provides
a graphic illustration of this workforce conceptualization—one with a
linear conception of the workforce that does not capture the networked
aspects of multiparty relationships.

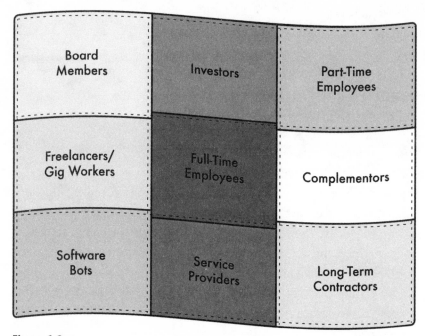

Figure 1.2
Workforce patchwork conceptualization.

Workforce as a Patchwork

We also heard workforces referred to as *patchworks*. This term evokes an image of a flowing quilt comprised of various fabrics that individually don't function well as a covering, but when stitched together create an effective item (see figure 1.2). Like the continuum analogy, this conceptualization has shortcomings; for instance, each element in a patchwork can only connect with those directly adjacent to it, and most elements are roughly the same size. Still, it helps expand our thinking to include a diverse array of interconnected elements. Catherine Popper of Launchpad Venture Group is an angel investor who works with entrepreneurs as they strive to build their businesses and gather the necessary resources. When asked how she defines a workforce, she responds, "I do feel like it's a bit of a patchwork these days. You end up thinking about all the various ways you can use talent: part-time, temps, the Upworks, the agencies, the remote developers. Everybody is using a little bit of everything. . . . There's a whole ecosystem of resources that are available."

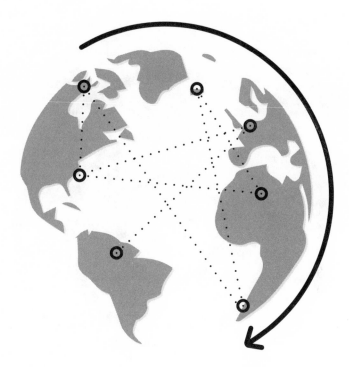

Figure 1.3
Workforce community conceptualization.

Workforce as a Community

Many companies today are keeping their core internal employee base as lean as possible while engaging with large communities of contributors, frequently in order to foster innovation. In some cases, these community members receive monetary compensation; in others, they are essentially volunteers interested in building their reputations, gaining experience, or simply having fun. Often, members join communities to take part in training or see what is happening with an organization, but never actually participate in a paid project. Applause Executive Chairman Reuveni describes his company's workforce structure in terms of a global community as it relies almost exclusively on contributors around the world to serve its clients (see figure 1.3).

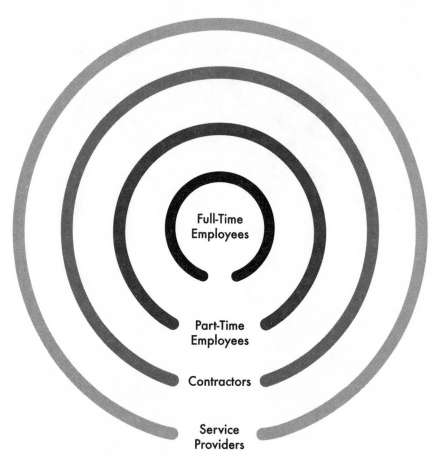

Figure 1.4
Workforce concentric circle conceptualization.

Workforce as Concentric Circles

Conceptualizing a workforce as concentric circles highlights the inclusion of various types of internal and external contributors. In this analogy, full-time internal employees are at the center, part-time employees are in the next ring, and contractors, professional services firms, and others occupy subsequent outer rings (see figure 1.4). The connections and networks among the different types of workers aren't evident in this analogy, but it does help leaders think about a workforce more holistically and how various programs may or may not apply to each type of worker. For example, a bonus program might only be relevant for the innermost circle while a training class or development opportunity might be available to a variety of rings all the way out to the edge. When asked how she defines a workforce, Jacqui Canney described it this way: "It's the entire network; all the rings. We're not going to just think about the inner ring of people. We're going to think about the outer rings—all of the people we hire who touch our business represent our workforce."

Action Questions

With an expansive view of the workforce, new connections are being created between employees and a broad range of external contributors. Building, maintaining, and managing these connections is no easy task. To begin, ask the following questions:

1. How do you define a workforce today?
2. Who and what do you believe is included in an organization's extended workforce?
   - Has this changed in the past one, two, or three years?
   - To what extent do you see the composition of workforces changing in the coming years?
3. If you work in an organization, are you prepared for changes in your extended workforce composition? What actions should you take to prepare for such shifts? More generally, what actions do you believe organizations should be taking to prepare?

2 What Is a Workforce Ecosystem?

Today's markets are global and interconnected, with interdependencies between suppliers, customers, partners, and other stakeholders. Since the early 1990s—beginning with the work of James Moore, Marco Iansiti, and others, and continuing with research by Ron Adner, Rahul Kapoor, and Carmelo Cennamo—authors, executives, consultants, and academics have considered biological ecosystems apt metaphors for the complex relationships characterizing today's business environment.[1] Referred to often as *business ecosystems*, and sometimes more specifically as *innovation ecosystems* or *networks of ecosystems*, these models capture how organizations interact with each other to accomplish separate and joint goals.[2]

In most writing on business-related ecosystems, however, the organizations themselves are considered to be black boxes. We don't often see what is happening *inside* any given company as we study ecosystems. With companies moving to a more open view of who is working for and with them, and workers and organizations reconsidering how they engage with companies, a black box no longer serves to represent the extensively networked twenty-first-century organization.

Workforce ecosystems represent a new way of conceptualizing an organization's relationships with various types of workers involved in creating value. These structures certainly encompass an organization's employees, but then go further to include external workers such as short- and long-term contractors, professional service firms, subcontractors, application developers, accessory providers, crowdsourcing participants, and even technologies. All of these contributors work toward accomplishing individual and organizational goals while serving customers of many types.

Elizabeth Adefioye, chief people officer of Emerson, a global technology and engineering company, observes,

> You can segment your workforce, of course, but I don't believe the worker is just the people who are full-time employees or people who are employed by the company and sitting on the payroll, because you have to think more broadly about how the work gets done. . . . You have temporary workers, you have contingent workers, you have consultants, you have those who are full-time employees, you have those who are job sharing, those who are part-time, those who are coming once in a while. . . . We have to be prepared for all of those types of workers because they bring different value. They create value differently. And quite frankly, if you want to be competitive in this world of work, you have to embrace all of those segments of workers.

A common understanding of workforce ecosystems will be helpful as managers learn more and communicate with their teams about them. Our definition builds on recent management theory research and our own research on the future of the workforce.[3] As we discussed in the introduction, we define a workforce ecosystem as:

> *A workforce ecosystem is a structure that encompasses actors, from within the organization and beyond, working to create value for an organization. Within the ecosystem, actors work toward individual and collective goals with interdependencies and complementarities among the participants.*[4]

Let's unpack each piece of this definition.

Workforce Ecosystems Are Structures

We call a workforce ecosystem a *structure*. In management research, *governance structures* refer to "formal and informal rules and procedures that control resource accumulation, development, and allocation."[5] In other words, governance structures consider how organizations organize themselves. In the case of workforce ecosystems, we look at not only organizations and their employees but also organizations and their relationships with external contributors. Some researchers would call this structure a *hybrid governance form* since it includes elements that are both part of an internal hierarchy (the organization) and a market (the external environment). In this book, we are interested in the whole system including internal contributors (full- and part-time employees) and external participants; most importantly, we are interested in their relationships with each other and how they all work together.[6]

Workforce Ecosystems Create Value

In our definition, we highlight a focus on *value creation*. We want to emphasize that workforce ecosystems exist to reach the strategic goals and objectives of organizations. We care most about how these structures operate to create value for all of an organization's stakeholders, including employees, contractors, gig workers, third-party contributors, customers, and investors.

Workforce Ecosystems Consist of Internal and External Participants

Workforce ecosystems include participants both *within and outside an organization*. Here, we will take a moment to elaborate on how we classify "internal" and "external" participants in this book.

By *internal*, we mean employees or individuals employed by an organization—full- or part-time, and either hourly or salary—generally with the intention that they will stay for some reasonably significant amount of time. These people usually (though not always, and this varies by geography) receive benefits such as medical insurance and retirement savings opportunities, and are covered by labor laws governing employee protections. Internal workers do not necessarily need to work within an organization's facilities. They may work remotely; physical location does not determine whether or not a worker is internal, employment does. Internal workers today can also refer to technologies like software bots (software programs that perform tasks) or automation robots.[7]

By *external*, we mean entities that are individuals who are not employees and organizations that do not reside within an organization's hierarchy. These entities contribute in some way to the value created by the organization at the center of the workforce ecosystem. Both long- and short-term contractors, for example, are external contributors, even if they physically work within the walls of an organization. We've seen that beyond its 110,000 employees, Novartis has roughly 50,000 people it considers to be external workers, and this number is growing. Note that some of these workers may work inside Novartis facilities and some may work remotely, but all are considered to be "external" since they are *not employees* of Novartis.

External participants aren't only individual contributors; they can be teams or organizations as well. As we've seen, Doron Reuveni of Applause leads the board of a company incorporating a worldwide community of over one million professional software testers. He explains, "As we look at that platform from a technology perspective, we're actually expanding it to include other teams. We have, for example, a feature called 'Bring Your Own Testers,' where you can say, 'OK, if I have another distributed team somewhere in India, I can have them join.'" Additionally, while software bots and other technologies owned by an organization might be considered internal, leased or contracted technologies might be considered external.

Workforce Ecosystems Encompass Individual and Collective Goals

Goals that workforce ecosystem participants aim to achieve should be both *individual* to them and *shared* with the central organization. By including both individual and collective goals in our definition, we recognize that participants are independent, with their own goals and objectives, while they also work toward goals that benefit the central organization or meet broader ecosystem-level objectives.

This duality of goals should hold true for both internal and external contributors. For instance, individual employees not only strive to achieve goals for the organization but have their own aspirations too, such as career progression, financial security, social fulfillment, and so on. External parties also have goals independent of the central organization. For example, an application developer creating an app for a smartphone may be a small company aiming to be acquired by a larger one. By participating in a workforce ecosystem (such as Apple's developer community), the developer might grow its company large enough to become an acquisition target. By recognizing that workforce ecosystem participants have both individual and collective goals, we remind ourselves that successfully managing a workforce ecosystem requires an organization to consider not only its own goals and objectives but also those of its ecosystem members.

Workforce Ecosystems Involve Interdependencies

Interdependencies are essential to workforce ecosystems. They reflect the interconnectedness inherent in workforce ecosystems, and highlight that members of the ecosystem either succeed or fail together. The success of an individual part of the ecosystem may depend on the success of other members of the system. The entire ecosystem is only able to accomplish its joint goals and objectives by not only including many types of participants but also ensuring that they can build relationships and work together.

Robert Gibbs, associate administrator, mission support at NASA, explains that the agency has a broad and inclusive workforce consisting of groups that need to work together to accomplish NASA's mission. "NASA is about one-third US federal employees—the traditional definition of the workforce in the federal government—and two-thirds contractors. But the way we look at it is that these are all NASA employees. In that external two-thirds, we also have 150 international partnerships and 2,600 commercial partnerships with 700 of them commencing annually across the agency. We do a lot of work across a lot of different spheres, and we try to make sure that we leverage the talents across this nontraditional definition of *workforce* to the best of our ability."

Jared Mueller of the Mayo Clinic provides another example from the medical center's Innovation Exchange, which connects researchers from around the world, many of whom are entrepreneurs, with medical researchers at Mayo.[8] He notes, "If we get to introduce people who are leaders in their fields, who, for example, happen to have started a small company in addition to being a prominent leader, then we can cross-pollinate and work on research agendas that way."

Without these relationships that span workforce ecosystems and include participants relying on each other's work, these world-class research organizations would not be able to reach their strategic goals. Many of their researchers depend on other members of their workforce ecosystems to provide expertise and innovative contributions.

Workforce Ecosystems Include Complementarities

In addition to interdependencies, we include *complementarities* in the definition. Truth be told, in our first article on workforce ecosystems we omitted complementarities because we thought they added unnecessary complexity. As we continued to speak with leaders, analyze our data, and learn more about these structures, however, we recognized that complementarities play a meaningful role in workforce ecosystems.

In short, complementarities exist when independent entities together provide value to customers. An oft-used example is a hot dog and hot dog bun. Both are likely made by different companies and sold separately to a customer, but together they deliver more value than either would supply alone. Very often, members of workforce ecosystems are complementors, meaning that they might not be contractually related to an organization as, say, suppliers, but they may be adding substantial value to an organization's products or services by creating products or offering services that work with them.[9] Take smartphone applications: the value of smartphones increases dramatically when software apps are added, even though most apps are not created by the phone or OS companies themselves. For example, a Samsung Android smartphone may become more valuable to a consumer when the game *Grand Theft*

Auto, published by Rockstar Games, is added to it. So Rockstar Games is a complementor to Samsung. Rockstar developers could be considered within Samsung's workforce ecosystem because their work enhances Samsung's products.

Connected fitness equipment provides another case. Peloton sells a bike with a full suite of content and functionality to connect its user community. A group of enthusiastic Peloton users, not Peloton employees, created a community within the community dedicated to maximizing training with Peloton's Power Zone classes, a specific type of spinning class. The independently operated PowerZonePack.com website and app (PZP) offer additional value to Peloton users by providing structured multiweek challenges and extensive ride data analysis. At last count, this wholly independent community of enthusiasts numbered over forty-five thousand riders.

PZP presents the classic double-edged sword problem of complementors for companies. On the positive side for Peloton, riders' engagement with the PZP community increases the likelihood that they will continue paying Peloton's monthly membership subscriptions. On the negative side, PZP subscribers are paying supplemental membership fees to PZP, buying T-shirts from PZP, and building loyalty to a separate brand, potentially costing Peloton lost revenue. Still, Peloton sees the value in this avid user community, and the company enables PZP by allowing the PZP app to gather Peloton user data from its systems. Peloton recognizes that the leaders of this extended community are essentially part of its workforce ecosystem: while the people running PZP are not Peloton employees, they are complementors to Peloton; they are working for the benefit of Peloton while also benefiting themselves.

Workforce Ecosystems Often Connect with Other Workforce Ecosystems

Up until now, we have discussed workforce ecosystems as if they were independent entities. But workforce ecosystems frequently exist as parts of larger systems that may be chains or nested ecosystems, where ecosystems associated with different organizations may develop relationships with each other.

Imagine that a firm with its own workforce ecosystem becomes part of another firm's workforce ecosystem. One company we studied operates in 110 countries and has over 100,000 employees. Their CHRO explained to us that recently two of their clients asked whether the company could loan them a few senior people to fill key roles in the short term. The CHRO explains, "If there are openings in some of the critical places in their functions, they can spin our people into those seats for six, twelve, or eighteen months." In cases like this, the company's employees can become part of a client's ecosystem; they can become the external workers.

Alternatives to Workforce Ecosystems

When we talk about workforce ecosystems with executives, consultants, and researchers, they occasionally highlight other structures and ask how they differ from workforce ecosystems. In this section, we compare and contrast workforce ecosystems with related structures.

Supply Chains

Generally speaking, when one refers to a business supply chain—sometimes also called a value system—one considers the myriad vendors that supply ingredient parts to an organization to produce and deliver a product or service. (Discussions of supply chains often focus on their vulnerability to disruption.)[10] These chains are usually modeled as linear systems with flows of inputs and outputs; an oft-used analogy is a flowing river with upstream and downstream movement. In contrast, workforce ecosystems are a more dispersed networked structure with connections and relationships that are frequently nonlinear, and are not necessarily formalized through extensive contracts. As they encompass complementor communities, for example, they often include contributors that are not contractually linked with the central company (e.g., an app developer or crowdsourcing contributor), or if they are it may be through a very standardized boilerplate (or "click-through") contract or license. It is true that in many cases, supply chain organizations, such as procurement departments, have responsibility for engaging parts of workforce ecosystems through managing relationships with talent agencies or labor platforms as well as arranging contingent labor. Still, though technically we could consider the delivery of labor a supply input, for our purposes, it is more useful for managers to consider labor inputs, especially when they are humans, as members of a workforce ecosystem rather than as goods delivered through a supply chain.

Alliances, Joint Ventures, and Consortia

Similarly, there is not a simple distinction between other types of interorganizational relationships and workforce ecosystems. Within a workforce ecosystem, there may be interorganizational relationships that could be strategic alliances or partnerships. We find it useful, however, to consider these in the broader context of an ecosystem governance structure, especially when they are part of larger initiatives toward reaching strategic goals. Sometimes these relationships though are not truly part of a workforce ecosystem at all. Alliances, generally speaking, are between two organizations, and often tied to specific desired business outcomes that it may or may not make sense to consider as part of a workforce ecosystem. For example, in 2020, Polaris, a $7 billion maker of outdoor sports vehicles such as off-road vehicles and snowmobiles, partnered with Zero Motorcycles, an electric motorcycle and power train company, for a ten-year exclusive deal to incorporate Zero's power trains into Polaris's products.[11] In this relationship, the companies will work together to codevelop technologies and vehicles; thus Zero, though remaining independent, could be considered part of Polaris's workforce ecosystem. By contrast, in 2015, the Brazilian footwear company Havaianas announced a strategic alliance with Disney to create Disney-themed flip-flops and sell its footwear at Disney properties.[12] While this relationship was particularly beneficial for Havaianas, allowing the company to sell more flip-flops, and good for Disney too, promoting Disney characters and films, Havaianas did not really become part of Disney's workforce ecosystem since its flip-flops were produced and sold separately from Disney products. Havaianas, while certainly a valuable partner, was not a complementor or playing a role we would consider to be part of a workforce ecosystem.

Through different legal structures, joint ventures result in the creation of a third legal entity, resulting in a new blended organization. This new entity might become part of one (or both) of the parent companies' workforce ecosystems if the products or services are inputs or complementors. If they are producing an entirely separate product, potentially even in a completely different industry, they might not.

Consortia (including standard-setting organizations) usually involve member groups all working toward a collective goal; they often include competitors working on standard setting or precompetitive research.[13] These communities work together on shared objectives; they are generally not orchestrated by a central organization interested primarily in furthering its own competitive goals.

In sum, all of these constructs are used to explain relationships between organizations, and some might be helpful in identifying subsets of workforce ecosystems. But none of them captures all the characteristics and dynamics that we are able to explore through a workforce ecosystem structure.

Action Questions

1. Consider an organization where you work or that you would like to analyze. Does this organization have a workforce ecosystem?
   - Is the leadership team managing the workforce as an ecosystem or is it focused primarily on employees?
   - If the organization has a workforce ecosystem, can you explain how the workforce ecosystem meets the various elements of the definition?
2. What benefits (if any) are possible from the organization taking a more integrated approach to managing employees and external contributors?
3. Who should be involved in a discussion that advances the pursuit of these benefits?

3   Strategy and Workforce Ecosystems

"True competitive differentiation comes from understanding the total workforce," Banyan Software's Arun Srinivasan observes. By providing easier access to all types of work participants, and offering a more holistic view across an organization and its network of contributors, workforce ecosystems facilitate this valuable understanding and ability to engage with the total or extended workforce.

The focus on the extended workforce represents a significant shift from how executives have typically viewed workforce planning. Workforce discussions often revolve around strategy implementation, on how organizations can acquire and deploy the resources necessary to achieve a previously determined set of strategic goals and objectives.

With workforce ecosystems, new strategic options become possible, and the process of discovering these options also changes. If top leaders are uncertain about how or whether to enter an emerging market because they lack crucial insights, workforce ecosystems can help to uncover those insights. If leaders want to build a strategy that relies on artificial intelligence (AI), for example, but worry about acquiring necessary data scientists and data, workforce ecosystems can help make that strategy more feasible. By allowing companies to more flexibly access a range of contributors of various types, workforce ecosystems enable new strategic avenues.

Elevating workforce ecosystems to play a strategic role depends in part on the kind of workforce ecosystem you have or aspire to have. Workforce ecosystems have specific characteristics that can inform and support both strategic planning and execution. Understanding these characteristics and deciding how to cultivate them are essential to developing workforce ecosystems that can expand strategic options.

This chapter has two main sections. The first offers a perspective on business strategy and how it intersects with the role of workforce ecosystems for organizations. The second introduces a set of research-derived workforce ecosystem characteristics that help us better understand and categorize different types of workforce ecosystems. Essentially, workforce ecosystems can take various forms; understanding these forms helps us to determine how best to link strategy discussions with workforce ecosystems.

Strategy and Workforce Ecosystems

A Perspective on Strategy

Strategy professors, business strategists, and executives all have their favorite approaches to strategy, which vary depending on one's background and set of experiences. Some strategists place great emphasis on industry analysis and competitive positioning. Others are heavily economics and finance based, using various formulae to calculate available market sizes and shifts over time. Still others are interested in how organizations can manage themselves to be most innovative and growth oriented. All of these perspectives boil down to decision-making and trade-off analysis; all at some point must address feasibility. Workforce ecosystems can play a role in these strategy conversations as they magnify the capabilities available to an organization.

An overwhelming majority of survey respondents—91 percent—agree or strongly agree that upcoming changes to their organization's business strategy require it to improve access to new capabilities, skill sets, and competencies. That broad agreement suggests that workforce ecosystems are a strategy-level discussion. Walmart's Donna Morris concurs, arguing that HR ought to have a more strategic role. "HR should work hand-in-hand with the business strategy officer or chief operating officer and CEO to determine where the business is going," she says.

"Do you have the right organization design? Do you have the right roles in the right locations at the right cost levels? What's in-house? What's outside?"

The best strategy discussions take a cross-operational view, considering choices affecting multiple functional areas. If a decision is far-reaching enough to affect not only HR but also marketing, research and development, finance, IT, manufacturing, sales, and so on, it is more likely to be a strategic one. The approach to workforce ecosystems that we advocate in this book similarly takes a cross-functional view, highlighting the value in coordinating work-related relationships (both employee based and with external contributors) across an organization. For example, if a company wants to move into a new region, the most expeditious way may be to start with a local partnership that includes collaboration between employees and external contributors across a range of functional areas.

Strategic decision-making also addresses an organization's competitive environment. What is the industry or market in which the organization is currently operating, and how is this likely to change? Who are, and will be, the most threatening competitors? Again, workforce ecosystems play a role since they can expeditiously enable an organization to move into an adjacent or entirely new market. Similarly, if a business intends to expand the functionality of a product or service, it might make sense to engage contractors for localization. More extensively, if a company recognizes that one of its products might benefit from the addition of apps or accessories, it may open interfaces and launch an app store (or related e-commerce site) to encourage complementors to offer products that work with its own. In all of these examples, workforce ecosystems can help a business improve its standing in relation to its competition.

Finally, strategic decisions tend to be long-term. Novartis's Markus Graf underscores the significance of an extended perspective. "There's a lot of data to help business leaders make sense of what they see today," he notes. "What's even more important is to help them see trends of what skills are becoming more important, less important, and then to

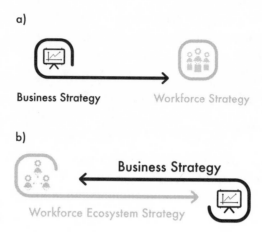

a)

Business Strategy   Workforce Strategy

b)

Business Strategy

Workforce Ecosystem Strategy

Figure 3.1
(a) Traditional business strategy drives workforce strategy. (b) Workforce ecosystem strategy informs business strategy and vice versa.

predict how the profile will look in three years. Just managing today is important, but managing for how the world will look in three to five years is critical."

Incorporating Workforce Ecosystem Strategy with Business Strategy

Business strategy decisions ordinarily drive workforce strategy decisions, such as how many people need to be hired, where they need to be placed, and what skills they need to have. Figure 3.1a represents the typical process.

Workforce ecosystems can dramatically alter this dynamic. As they become the predominant way for organizations to view how work gets done to achieve strategic goals and objectives, they can affect decision-making driving business strategy. What previously was a one-way practice can become much more dynamic and iterative, with workforce ecosystem strategy evolving in concert with business strategy, with each informing the other. Figure 3.1b illustrates this new reinforcing process.

While the practice is not yet widespread, a workforce ecosystem approach is well positioned to inform business strategy. Imperial College London's Christopher Tucci, professor of digital strategy and innovation, describes a "reverse causality" in which companies "create or influence strategy based on shifting the workforce toward more ecosystem thinking." Carmelo Cennamo, professor of strategy and entrepreneurship at Copenhagen Business School, expects a similar shift. He explains, "We tend to see the workforce as a top-down process. We set strategy; we have goals. Then it comes down to operations: 'We need these resources, and human capital is one. Do we have these people? No, let's hire them.' But the other way around—bottom-up—will be that the resources you have might actually push you to explore other directions. Some of this pool might be seen as a way to leverage innovation opportunities or strategic directions for the company itself."

Tobias Kretschmer, professor of management and head of the Institute for Strategy, Technology, and Organization at Ludwig-Maximilians-Universität München, sketches a scenario in which business strategy might be derived from the workforce ecosystem. "You have access to a much wider range of skills," he notes. "Let's say I'm a firm that wants to expand to a developing country. If I have temporary workers that have a deep knowledge of that market, I can get them to help me with analysis, with competitor assessment, with market entry strategy. This would have been prohibitively costly before because I would have had to hire someone for that country. To be able to get more fine-grained expertise allows implementation of more fine-grained strategies."

In sum, workforce ecosystems invite and inform strategic discussions. When particular skills and capabilities are available cost-effectively (either through direct engagement or by enabling complementors), and when they provide a sustainable competitive advantage, leaders can drive a company in a new direction. In that way, workforce ecosystems can influence business strategy.

Workforce Ecosystem Characteristics: The Three Cs

Workforce ecosystems vary in terms of size, scope, composition, relationships, and other dimensions. Some companies may use a workforce ecosystem model extensively, relying on contributors of various types across their organization. Others may only use external contributors and ecosystem-type relationships (with high interdependencies, for example) in select instances. Given their strategic potential, it's useful to identify different kinds of workforce ecosystems to determine which may be appropriate in which situation.

As workforce ecosystems increase in prevalence and relevance, we see the value in classifying their different types, and understanding how and why they differ. Once this is done, we can start to answer some key questions: When might one type of workforce ecosystem be more useful than another? Why might one adopt a particular type over another? While we remain in the early stages of this work, our research shows that three characteristics are sufficient to distinguish between types of workforce ecosystems.

We call these characteristics the Three Cs of workforce ecosystems: comprehensiveness, community, and coordination. Together, they provide a way to classify workforce ecosystems and understand how they differ (or possess commonalities).

Comprehensiveness

Comprehensiveness captures how extensive a workforce ecosystem is. Some organizations utilize business models developed entirely around a workforce ecosystem structure. Thus their workforce ecosystem will have a high degree of comprehensiveness. Applause is an example of this type of company: its ability to conduct its business relies entirely on a workforce ecosystem that encompasses external workers including both individuals and organizations. A company scoring low on comprehensiveness might be a large, mature incumbent organization focused primarily on internal employees while just starting to introduce external workers more deliberately into its workforce.

Organizations that exhibit high workforce ecosystem comprehensiveness are likely to have business strategies that rely heavily on the robustness of their workforce ecosystem. For instance, Applause cannot provide its primary offering of testing services without its global ecosystem of testers; it cannot reach any of its strategic goals without its workforce ecosystem. Its high workforce ecosystem comprehensiveness is at the heart of the organization.

Here are a few questions to start a conversation around the degree of comprehensiveness in a workforce ecosystem:

1. To what degree is your organization dependent on external contributors to reach its strategic goals and objectives?
   - To what extent does the organization have interdependencies with external parties?
   - What form do they usually take, if there is a typical form?
2. What types of external contributors does your organization engage? In what ways are they engaged? In what parts of the organization are they being leveraged?
3. What types of complementors does your organization have? Approximately how many does it have (even roughly an order of magnitude could be helpful: Ten? One hundred? A thousand? . . . Millions?)?

Community

Workforce ecosystems often include groups of contributors to an organization. These are frequently independent individuals or organizations doing specific work on a transactional basis. They may or may not extensively interact with members of the central organization, and may have no reason to interact with one another. In these cases, they may not feel like they are members of a community. In other instances, however, groups of contributors may interact extensively with an organization. They may feel very much like they are part of an extended organization. They may also interact with other external contributors and feel like they are part of a community of contributors. In these situations, the organization has created a feeling of commonality and shared experiences.

An organization's efforts, or lack thereof, to build a community (or communities) as part of its workforce ecosystem will affect how it interacts with and utilizes its workforce ecosystem. The level of community that an organization chooses to foster in its workforce ecosystem is part of its workforce ecosystem strategy. It may substantially inform and enable an organization's strategy. For example, Threadless, a T-shirt design company that researchers have studied for its reliance on a community of freelance designers, could not accomplish its primary strategic objective of offering custom printed T-shirts and other goods without its community of designers.[1] The designers communicate with each other, provide feedback on each other's designs, and vote on the best designs. In addition to building relationships with the central company, Threadless, they build relationships with each other, the community members.

Community building can introduce new challenges for workforce ecosystem management. In some cases, there might be a sense of first- and second-class citizenship between internal employees and external workers. In others, the borders between who (and what) is or isn't internal might be blurry. Still, organizations that are high on the community scale strive to make external workers feel like they are essential to the success of the central organization. They sometimes aim to incorporate external contributors into the culture of the company as well.

Interestingly, while we usually assume that organizations with communities deliberately set out to build those communities, that is not always the case. In some instances, organizations find themselves with communities that have arisen independently; at that point, they must decide whether and how to engage with them. For example, LEGO has an avid customer fan base that grew organically with the popularity of LEGO products. Beyond children, the company's markets expanded to include adults whose hobby was building with LEGOs. These customers started creating their own groups and gatherings to share information about LEGO and provide feedback to the company (for example AFOL, or Adult Fans of LEGO).[2] Complementors emerged that designed and sold accessory products like lights and stickers for LEGO sets. LEGO learned to embrace these communities, harnessing their enthusiasm for the company's benefit. LEGO is now high on the community scale as it actively nurtures and engages with various communities that have become critical to its business.

An interesting additional note is that we usually don't consider *customers* to be integral to workforce ecosystems. In the case of LEGO and others, however, customers play a pivotal role in providing input to the organization. In these situations, customers are essential members of a workforce ecosystem community, dramatically strengthening the power and strategic value of the ecosystem.

Here are some questions to begin to assess the community level in a workforce ecosystem:

1. To what degree has your organization built a community or communities as part of its workforce ecosystem?

2. To what extent are interactions with external contributors considered transactional versus community relationship building?

3. How differently are external workers treated from internal employees? Are there any shared benefits?

4. Do external workers consider themselves to be part of a community related to your organization? To what extent do they consider themselves to be part of the organization's culture? Do employees include them in that culture?

5. Do external contributors interact with each other in any way, beyond specific interactions with the organization? For instance, do they provide each other feedback on their contributions or rank each other?

Coordination

Coordination is the third characteristic and describes the extent to which an organization controls its workforce ecosystem. It has two elements. One encompasses topics that some might refer to as governance or functional jurisdictions. Within an organization, who is responsible for various relationships, and to what extent are these relationship management activities coordinated? If as is customarily the case, for example, HR is responsible for managing and tracking all full- and part-time employee hiring, and procurement is responsible for managing and tracking all contractor hiring, to what degree, if any, are these functions discussing these activities with each other? If a strategy group is responsible for the organization's most complex strategic alliances, and another group is responsible for developer relations, are they coordinating their activities? Each group is managing part of a workforce ecosystem. The coordination characteristic allows us to discuss how integrated these conversations might be.

Relatedly, organizations vary not only in which parts of the organization are managing different types of relationships but also in how, overall, they interact with external contributors. This aspect of coordination often manifests itself in questions about the degree of control an organization exerts in external relationships. For example, Google Play (formerly Android Market) is Google's distribution marketplace for apps and content. In comparison to Apple's App Store, through which Apple distributes apps and content, Google has a lighter touch, with less strict requirements and compliance testing. Apple's policies are known to be much more stringent. Thus we would say that Apple is more extensively coordinating its ecosystem than Google is.

For workforce ecosystems, in considering coordination, we can describe both the extent to which an organization is internally coordinated (how intentionally and effectively it is working cross-functionally on various types of relationship management) and how actively an organization is managing its external contributors. Both of these considerations inform strategic decision-making. Internally, an organization may need to decide which functions will interact with external providers, and how coordinated they plan to be as they handle those relationships. Looking outward, the extent of coordination with third parties or developers may determine the degree to which external organizations are willing to expend resources to participate in (or contribute to) the workforce ecosystem. Business history is littered with stories of organizations that didn't do well coordinating with developer ecosystems (e.g., Blackberry, formerly known as RIM).

We recognize that the coordination measure is broad in scope. Yet we believe that an expansive notion of coordination provides a good summarizing viewpoint of how an organization approaches management of the relationships within its workforce ecosystem.

Here are some questions to help assess the degree of coordination in a workforce ecosystem:

1. How holistic is the approach to workforce ecosystem management?
   - For example, are there consistent workforce ecosystem management practices across the organization?
   - How much cross-functional coordination is there between groups within the organization that are managing both internal and external contributors?
   - Are there formal systems in place, or regular meetings or other processes, that allow members of different groups to gain visibility to workforce ecosystem relationships that are managed outside their own organizations?
2. What forms of governance does your organization deploy in its relationships with participants in the workforce ecosystem? For example, is there strict compliance testing of some type?
3. To what extent is the workforce ecosystem centrally coordinated?

Dynamism of Workforce Ecosystems

So far we have discussed workforce ecosystems, their key characteristics (comprehensiveness, community, and coordination), and their relationships with strategy, all at static points in time. Workforce ecosystems and their characteristics are continually changing though, and that has an evolving impact on business strategy. Hence we should also take a dynamic perspective and consider how workforce ecosystems transform over time.

For example, when Apple first began creating iPod music players (before introducing smartphones), this was a new foray for the company into mobile music devices. Examining this enterprise through the Three Cs, we see that Apple had not yet built a workforce ecosystem that included both its own employees and also the companies creating speakers, headphones, cases, and the like that it needed to provide greater value to customers of its products. The workforce ecosystem was not yet *comprehensive*, and there was no *community* to speak of back then. Lastly, the ecosystem was not *coordinated*, as there were initially few accessory providers and Apple didn't yet have a team of people working across organizational boundaries to coordinate its internal employees with external contributors. Apple had started to work with accessory companies on a one-off basis, such as to build speakers, but it did not yet have a system in place for managing the ecosystem.

As Apple's success with music players, and then smartphones and tablets, grew, its workforce ecosystem related to these products grew as well. As of 2022, it would be more than fair to say that Apple's workforce ecosystem, and especially the accessory component of it, is highly comprehensive and coordinated. In terms of community, this is a harder question, as one could argue that Apple's relationship with accessory providers is mainly transactional and often arm's length. Still, Apple has an extensive program to manage these relationships called Mfi (formerly Made for iPod, iPhone, iPad).[3] Yet the company does not seem to aspire to create a functioning community among the members. In sum, we see that the Three Cs are useful for describing this case of a workforce ecosystem and its changes over time.

Here are some questions to assess the dynamism in a workforce ecosystem:

1. To what extent is your workforce ecosystem increasing or decreasing in comprehensiveness, community, and coordination?
2. How has it changed over the past one, two, three, or x number of years?
3. How do you expect it to change in the coming years?

Action Questions

In this chapter, we included questions for each characteristic in the text, so please refer to those sections for action questions associated with the Three Cs.

Here are a few questions related to workforce ecosystems and strategy. As you answer these, consider an organization where you work or that you would like to analyze.

1. Is there an opportunity in your organization to develop a workforce ecosystem strategy and have it play an integral role in influencing and refining business strategy? If not, what are the barriers, and can/should they be overcome?

2. Can a workforce ecosystem strategy influence the business strategy, and vice versa, in a symbiotic or mutually beneficial way? How? What resources are necessary to accomplish this? Over what time frame?

3. Are any competitors using workforce ecosystems?

   - To what extent are they doing so, and how are they structured?
   - If they are not now, do you expect that they will be soon? When?
   - How will this change the nature of competition in your industry and market?
   - Do differences between your workforce ecosystem and a competitor's put your organization at an advantage or disadvantage? Why and in what ways?

II Orchestrating Workforce Ecosystems

4 A Framework for Workforce Ecosystem Orchestration

Ask a manager how they manage their workforce, and you'll get an earful of wisdom, experience, and insight. Ask the same manager how to manage a workforce ecosystem, and you're as likely to receive hems and haws as you are a well-developed point of view.

Managing a workforce ecosystem—intentionally orchestrating all the players, inside and outside the organization, so that they are working together to advance an organization's strategy and purpose—is no small feat.

We use the term *orchestration*, not *management*, in part because management often implies or directly refers to control. In a system of contributors who may or may not be directly controlled by management, an optimal term should capture the agency or autonomy of a wide range of actors throughout the ecosystem. Ecosystem orchestration is an emerging phrase in both academic and leadership-focused business literature precisely due to this consideration. Workforce ecosystem orchestration conveys the idea that individual actors have agency or autonomy beyond the strictures imposed by HR and management fiat.

Orchestration can take many forms, as Reed Hastings and Erin Meyer explain in their book *No Rules Rules*.[1] Conducting a symphony orchestra consisting of many varied classical musicians involves leading individuals who have proscribed roles and have received extensive guidance about what they should be doing. Leading a jazz band, in contrast, entails creating the conditions to enable skilled musicians to embark on brilliant improvisation. Both orchestration activities can result in glorious performances, but the levels of control exerted and the approaches to managing the participants are quite different. Still, both cases involve assembling diverse contributors to create a complete outcome.

We use the term *orchestration* in this broad way to mean coordinating groups of participants to create an aligned effort toward meeting organizational (and individual) goals and objectives. In particular, as we do throughout this book, we focus on the organization at the center of the workforce ecosystem and its role in orchestrating its workforce ecosystem members, both internal and external.

A Workforce Ecosystem Orchestration Index: Intentional Orchestration

We developed a measurement system to determine how far along an organization might be on a path to more intentionally orchestrating its workforce ecosystem. The question we were setting out to answer is what, if anything, differentiates organizations that are further along in the process from those that are not. We used our survey data to develop what we call a *workforce orchestration index* that groups organizations into three categories: intentional orchestrators, partial orchestrators, and nonorchestrators. These categories reflect to what degree an organization is intentionally leading and managing its workforce ecosystem.

We used three criteria to differentiate between these categories, reflecting the answers to the following questions:

1. To what extent does the organization have a vision of the workforce that includes both internal and external contributors?
2. To what extent is the management of internal and external workers integrated?
3. What is the degree of preparedness for managing a workforce made up of more external providers?

From organizations' scores on these questions, we calculated an index score that we then mapped to our three categories. From there, we looked at how these different categories of organizations fared on other survey questions. We recognized that intentional orchestrators tend to have several particular attributes. They are more likely to closely coordinate the cross-functional management of internal and external workers as well as third-party organizations; hire and engage the internal and external talent they need; support managers seeking to hire external workers and engage with external collaborators; have leadership that understands how to allocate work for internal and external workers and collaborators; and align their workforce approach with their business strategy.

By way of example, Novartis is an organization that scores high on the index and thus we consider to be an intentional orchestrator. It is explicitly coordinating the cross-functional management of internal and external workers, and supporting managers hiring external workers. Discussing the integration of Novartis's 110,000 internal workers with its approximately 50,000 external workers, Markus Graf explains, "The mix has been shifting toward more external and fewer internal people on our own payroll. So it requires us to think, in terms of processes and technology enablement, 'How do we tap into this pool of external resources?'"

An Orchestration Framework for Workforce Ecosystems

Workforce ecosystem orchestration is not just an HR responsibility. Senior leaders and business unit leaders also make decisions related to managing a workforce ecosystem as do leaders in HR, procurement, IT, finance, legal, and other groups.

From our research, we have identified four themes that are helpful and arguably essential to consider as one strives to orchestrate a workforce ecosystem: *leadership approaches, integration architectures, technology enablers*, and *management practices*. We explain these in more detail below.

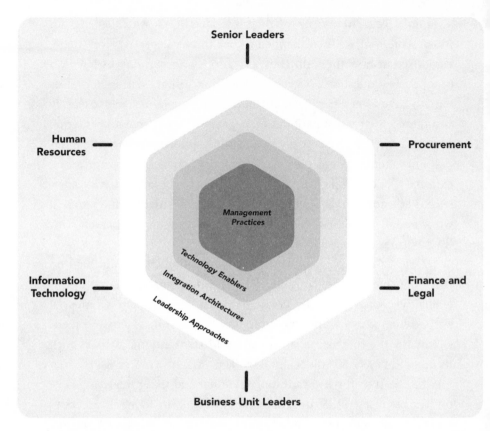

Figure 4.1
Workforce ecosystem orchestration framework.

Considering the sets of players working to orchestrate workforce eco-systems and these recurring themes, we developed a *workforce ecosystem orchestration framework* (see figure 4.1).

The framework illustrates how organizational functions come together in a workforce ecosystem, and building on our identified themes, addresses key activities and systems essential to workforce eco-system orchestration. Around the outside of the figure are the critical players, including senior leadership, business unit leaders, and func-tional areas. We organize these along three axes. We place *senior leaders* and *business unit leaders* on the vertical axis through the middle of the figure because these are primary orchestrators who generally need to take a holistic and integrated view of the ecosystem. We place *human resources* and *procurement* opposite each other on the top horizontal axis through the figure because these functions often have managerial responsibilities associated with gaining access to as well as managing essential contributors to the ecosystem. We place *information technology* across from *finance and legal* on the second horizontal axis through the figure to represent functions that serve crucial roles to enable the ecosystem to exist and operate effectively.

The four concentric hexagons depicted in figure 4.1 correspond to the themes that emerged from our research encompassing cross-functional activities and systems vital to orchestrating workforce ecosystems.

The outermost hexagon in the figure represents *leadership approaches*. Orchestrating workforce ecosystems requires significant shifts in leadership behaviors and mindsets. For instance, since many participants in workforce ecosystems are external to the company—such as gig workers, subcontractors, and app developers—managers cannot exert the same types of direct control that they can with their own employees. As additional examples, in a workforce ecosystem, community building within and beyond organizational boundaries and influencing without control become critical elements of a leader's toolbox. Furthermore, DE&I principles and practices are examples of organizational elements that may need to be extended to apply to external contributors. Leaders across all levels and functions have to reevaluate what it means for them to lead in a workforce ecosystem structure. Chapter 5 delves more deeply into these topics.

The next hexagon in the figure represents *integration architectures* related to orchestrating workforce ecosystems. Within an organization, functional areas and business units need to work together differently in workforce ecosystems. We hear time and again from executives who see redundancies, gaps, and conflicts in how their organizations engage both employees and external workers. In some cases, different parts of organizations manage different types of ecosystem relationships. A business development group, for example, might be responsible for strategic partnerships, whereas another group might own developer relations; without an integrated approach, this could lead to internal tensions and confused messaging to third parties. Integration architectures span not only HR and procurement (for accessing external talent) but also other areas, including IT (for data access, for instance), legal (for contracting), and finance (for allocations, invoicing, and payments). Finally, leaders must decide how they should coordinate relationships with external contributors—such as choosing how rigorously they want to control third-party outcomes (say, deciding to what extent they will provide strict or not so strict compliance testing for software apps). We discuss integration architectures in more detail in chapter 6.

The following concentric hexagon, *technology enablers*, represents the information systems and data that enable the management of all types of contributors. In most organizations, workforce-related technologies and data are fragmented; different systems in different silos apply to different workforce contributors. One system might track contract labor within one functional area (such as IT), while another might manage a developer ecosystem that creates apps that augment a product's functionality. Yet another system might track third-party distribution subcontractors. Orchestrating workforce ecosystems includes managing and connecting the technologies that serve both the organization and its different types of contributors. In chapter 7, we present five roles that technologies play in shaping, supporting, and participating in workforce ecosystems.

In the center of the figure illustrating our orchestration framework is a hexagon that symbolizes *management practices*. Workforce ecosystems require fundamental shifts in how organizations approach some of their key practices. For example, many management practices are tied to the so-called employee life cycle model: acquiring, developing, and retaining full-time employees. In a workforce ecosystem, new management practices are often required to attract the best talent available, wherever it is, and engage individuals and organizations via various types of relationships (such as finding individual contributors through digital labor platforms, or by opening interfaces and enabling software developers to create apps to offer in app stores).

The next four chapters detail how orchestrating workforce ecosystems can address issues that arise in each of the four hexagons. The chapters discuss each of the themes encompassed by the hexagons and provide examples of how these subject areas affect and are affected by each of the functional areas.

Action Questions

1. To what extent would it be valuable for your organization to have an overarching view of its entire workforce ecosystem?

2. Does your organization's leadership have a vision of the workforce that includes both internal and external contributors?

3. Is your organization preparing to manage a workforce composed of larger numbers of external contributors? Will these constitute a larger percentage of the overall workforce, and if so, are there preparations the organization should be making to address this shift?

5   Leadership Approaches in Workforce Ecosystems

We're going to have a different kind of leader in the future than we have today.

—Jacqui Canney, ServiceNow

Eighty percent of the skills, mindsets, attitudes, and behaviors that make for effective leadership will be the same as always, but 20 percent need to change.

—Tomas Chamorro-Premuzic, ManpowerGroup

The leadership skills, practices, and perspectives associated with orchestrating a workforce ecosystem represent a significant departure from those required in a hierarchical organization. Traditional organizations are predominantly composed of long-term employees engaged in somewhat stable jobs with annual performance metrics. Leaders orchestrating workforce ecosystems, on the other hand, recognize that these new, more complex structures—replete with different types of workers, employment models, and work environments—impose new demands on leadership.

The workforce ecosystem orchestration framework introduced in chapter 4 includes a hexagon representing leadership approaches that encompasses the shifts encountered by leaders who are orchestrating workforce ecosystems (see figure 5.1). The workforce ecosystem orchestration framework includes senior leaders at the top of the figure and business unit leaders at the bottom. We included these categories to

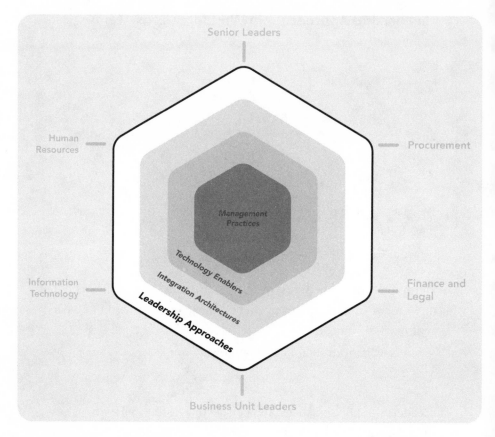

Figure 5.1
Leadership approaches in the workforce ecosystem orchestration framework.

highlight the pivotal roles played by an organization's most senior leaders, often the C-suite, and business unit leaders who are frequently tasked with operationalizing the day-to-day requirements of workforce ecosystem orchestration. The other functions represented in the hexagon diagram—human resources, procurement, information technology, and finance and legal—also include key leaders going through their own orchestration-related leadership shifts.

As leaders orchestrate workforce ecosystems, they will find that shifts in both their behaviors and mindsets are in order. The following sections highlight the most prominent of these shifts.

Relinquishing Direct Control

What's the best way to lead and manage a varied type of workforce to deliver the outcomes the end customer expects . . . if it's not directly within your control?

—Donna Morris, Walmart

For more than one hundred years, starting with the publication of Frederick Taylor's classic book *The Principles of Scientific Management* in 1911, organizational leadership has focused on controlling work and workers.[1] A key assumption is that employees do most, if not all, of the work in an organization. They conduct the work through standard processes that include jobs, roles, and tasks.

Leading in a workforce ecosystem embraces new assumptions: internal employees may or may not do most, or all, of the work. Jobs, roles, and tasks may be less standardized. Market mechanisms rather than job descriptions may assign labor to projects. Work *in* an organization broadens to work *for* an organization. Leaders recognize these shifts and that they need to adjust in response.

Our interviews unearthed a wide range of views from leaders about how they need to adjust their behaviors and mindsets to orchestrate, not control, their workforce ecosystems. They mentioned a renewed focus on resilience, trust, courage, digital savviness, and purpose. But one theme stood out above all others: leaders' relationship with control.

In more traditional structures, leaders have a variety of tools to directly control employees. They can grant new titles, provide perks, alter compensation, and so on, all in an effort to influence employee behavior. Not inconsequentially, employees are acutely aware that leaders have these levers within their power. As organizations evolve to operate through workforce ecosystems, however, leaders' reliance on direct control no longer serves them well. It is more difficult to control all the work of participants in an ecosystem structure. Moreover, when all is working well and interests are aligned, there's less reason to attempt to do so.

Accordingly, Paul Estes, founder of XpertLinkAI, an on-demand customer enablement platform, and former chief community officer at the digital collaboration platform Mural, advises leaders to give up trying:

> Say you spend a million dollars on freelancers—that's a ton of different people interacting with your organization. You can't micromanage it. There's a mindset of management that's like, "I have to control. I sit at the head of the table." Instead, you have to provide strategic vision, you have to unblock things, you have to make sure people understand the rules and build culture, and that's a different type of management because you can't control it. You have to empower the edges.

That difference, Estes believes, is threatening to many leaders. "Their entire value was, 'How many people report to me?' They're trying to manage up. When I started working with freelance teams, I stopped. I just wanted to do the work, I wanted to help the team. It changed how I led, and it changed me from being a coach to a player-coach." Relinquishing control doesn't mean relinquishing accountability, but it might entail the development of new tools and approaches to hold workers accountable for achieving desired outcomes.

Relinquishing control is not only a matter that arises when leading groups of external contributors but also is a feature of leadership efforts to increase the free flow of talent within an enterprise. Managers working within an ecosystem context, often enabled through marketplaces, lose control as workers gain access to more opportunities. Still, the organization benefits from more engaged workers who are continuing to upgrade their capabilities. Andrew Saidy, formerly global head of talent and learning at data storage company Seagate and now vice president of global talent at Ubisoft, describes reactions to his efforts to launch a talent marketplace, which can serve as an internal platform for matching people to roles based on skills, interests, and preferences.[2] He admits that

> there was pushback for a talent marketplace because it was very disruptive to the way we've always done things. In a traditional organization, if you have a superstar on your team, managers would want to hold on to them: "I don't want Liz to go anywhere." And then you block Liz from moving internally.

With the talent marketplace, Liz now has options. And one day, she could move. That takes power away from managers because they're no longer making career decisions on behalf of others and gives it to employees who now truly own their careers. The relationship between the marketplace and managers could be quite rocky, but we have done a lot to educate managers. It's complicated, but when you get there, it is definitely very gratifying.

Similarly, Julie Derene, senior vice president of global talent management at cloud-based human capital management software company Ceridian, agrees. "We need managers and leaders to be willing to help people see their way around the organization," says Derene, who refers to the mindset shift as "letting go of a 'my best talent mentality' and adopting more of an 'in the best interest of the company talent mentality.'" Chief human resources officer (CHRO) Susan Tohyama adds, "In principle, most managers will say, 'Oh, of course, whatever's in the best interest of my employee.' When it comes down to it, they're thinking, 'Hold up, I need this person. I don't want them to go over there.' That shift must happen." As leaders expand their perspectives on appropriate paths for their employees and other contributors, they also begin to see the advantages of opening these routes.

Still, talent sharing often represents a significant break from past practices tied to leading employees. Canney recalls that one of her previous clients in a former role had an internal "no-poaching policy" at one time:

> I thought it was a joke, but it was true. And if you did it, you could get fired. And that's a big barrier if you think you're going to get in trouble for asking someone to consider another role within your organization. It's critical that businesses see the value in advancing talent from within and across an organization. Enabling employees to build their careers internally leads to greater retention and engagement, and that is good for your people and good for your business.

Leaders who are considering their organizations holistically, and are also focused on the longer-term best interests of both their own organizations and the members of their workforce ecosystems, will be likely to adopt more indirect control mechanisms with more flexibility.

Dyan Finkhousen, chief strategy officer at Open Assembly, a network of consultants focused on future of work and open talent topics, believes that a mindset shift is necessary to share talent. "You need to have a mindset of abundance versus scarcity," she argues. "If you're thinking in a zero-sum game, and if you're used to taking a competitive posture versus a collaborative posture, you're not going to get very far. If you're hoarding intellectual property, if you're hoarding commercial opportunities, if you're hoarding information, you're not going to get very far." For many of these leaders, the transition to loosening control over workers while maintaining the integrity of the workflow depends on their adoption of a new view of how the workforce is structured—a challenge unto itself.

Relinquishing direct control not only facilitates more forward-thinking approaches to talent management but also supports a shift to leadership practices that are more appropriate in complex, highly interconnected structures such as workforce ecosystems. When managers don't have direct authority over all the workers contributing to accomplishing their strategic goals and objectives, they need to hone their skills of influence and persuasion. For example, in joint military operations, when service members come together from different branches, services, agencies, and countries, senior leaders must adopt more nuanced, influence-based leadership approaches that may be quite different from those they use within their own ranks.

Leadership development looks different in more open, networked workforce ecosystem models too; what makes sense in a hierarchical command-and-control context might not work in a workforce ecosystem model where leaders can exert much less control. For instance, much research has centered on the value of developing "T-shaped leaders" who have deep, specific functional or product expertise as well as broad organizational and/or industry knowledge. These types of leaders may be particularly adept at operating in a workforce ecosystem environment, which requires more subtle forms of persuasion and motivation of participants in an extended workforce. Developing leaders into T-shaped leaders could require new approaches, such as providing learning opportunities in other parts of the organization or offering access to opportunities outside the company that broaden their experiences.[3]

Finally, when contributors aren't hired as employees, leaders may not be able to offer them access to health care, retirement, childcare, or other benefits. Organizations can also be prevented by law from providing some opportunities, such as paid leave or developmental experiences, to workers who are legally classified as contractors. As we discuss in chapter 11, leaders are beginning to address the trade-offs that arise when they gain flexibility through contingent workers but are unable to offer those workers access to benefits. For now, suffice it to say that while leaders orchestrating workforce ecosystems can benefit by relinquishing some control as they gain the additional flexibility offered by an expanded workforce, they also encounter challenges that require thoughtful consideration and creative solutions that may reach well beyond their own organizations.

Leading across Organizational Boundaries

To be future fit, you need to galvanize leadership around a bigger goal than just managing your workforce internally.

—Jeroen Wels, Unilever (former)

Leaders in workforce ecosystems have the opportunity to think beyond the boundaries of their own organizations to leverage connections between their organizations and other contributors. How do the individual and organizational participants relate to one another? What are their dependencies? To what extent are they interdependent? Are there opportunities for complementarities?

In our 2020 global survey of executives, the vast majority of respondents—87 percent—included some external workers when considering their workforce composition.[4] We asked about several categories of workers, including full-time employees, contractors, service providers,

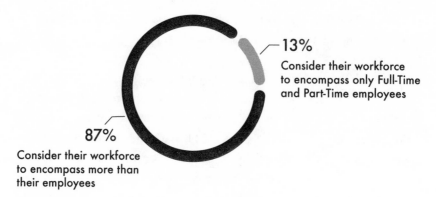

13%
Consider their workforce
to encompass only Full-Time
and Part-Time employees

87%
Consider their workforce
to encompass more than
their employees

Figure 5.2
A broader view of the workforce. *Note:* Percentages are based on 4,761 total
responses and exclude those who responded "don't know" or "not applicable."

developers, accessory providers, and technology. Among the 4,761
respondents, only 13 percent viewed their workforces strictly in terms
of employees. This more expansive workforce perspective suggests that
leaders need to consider the relationships between all of these participants (see figure 5.2).

Most executives recognize that their workforce composition extends
beyond employees; they anticipate that external contributors will
increase in the near term as well. Many expect growth across all categories of contributors, especially technologies like robots, chatbots, and
AI. Those with the broadest definition of the workforce expect to see
the strongest growth (see figure 5.3).

While executives recognize that workforce composition has changed,
and is changing, preparations for these shifts have by and large not
kept pace. Only 28 percent of the global respondents reported that
they are "sufficiently preparing to manage a workforce that will rely
more on external participants." This too adds challenges for leaders,
who must teach their managers to look beyond their own organizations
(see figure 5.4).

Leading teams composed of internal and external workers demands
a point of view about the meaning of *teamwork*. In some organizational

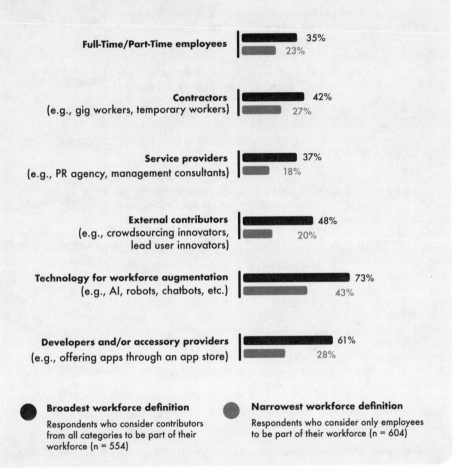

Respondents expect the following categories of workforce participants to increase over the next 18–24 months:

Full-Time/Part-Time employees — 35% / 23%

Contractors (e.g., gig workers, temporary workers) — 42% / 27%

Service providers (e.g., PR agency, management consultants) — 37% / 18%

External contributors (e.g., crowdsourcing innovators, lead user innovators) — 48% / 20%

Technology for workforce augmentation (e.g., AI, robots, chatbots, etc.) — 73% / 43%

Developers and/or accessory providers (e.g., offering apps through an app store) — 61% / 28%

Broadest workforce definition
Respondents who consider contributors from all categories to be part of their workforce (n = 554)

Narrowest workforce definition
Respondents who consider only employees to be part of their workforce (n = 604)

Figure 5.3
Workforce participation growth by category. *Note:* Percentage who agree and strongly agree; multiselect question; percentages do not total 100 percent.

Survey Respondents...

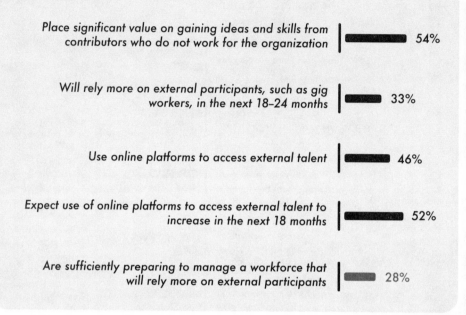

Place significant value on gaining ideas and skills from contributors who do not work for the organization — 54%

Will rely more on external participants, such as gig workers, in the next 18–24 months — 33%

Use online platforms to access external talent — 46%

Expect use of online platforms to access external talent to increase in the next 18 months — 52%

Are sufficiently preparing to manage a workforce that will rely more on external participants — 28%

Figure 5.4
Workforce ecosystem participation is increasing, yet preparation is lagging.

environments, everyone shares the same goal, such as to cure cancer or safely launch a rocket. In such situations, it is easier for everyone to work together as a unified team. At the Mayo Clinic, for example, Jared Mueller, who runs the medical center's Innovation Exchange, notes that they are resourcing support in previously untapped locations to provide high-quality care to patients who can't travel to Minnesota. (The pandemic obviously accelerated this goal.) This mandate, he points out, comes from the top.

"We're really lucky that we have a CEO who drives this institutional priority," Mueller says. "When you have a supreme value, which is that the needs of the patient come first, and you have leadership that both embraces that value and also drives home the need to be open to ideas from other institutions, from other countries, other bright minds in industry, or in other fields, you have the permission space to really keep pushing that with total comfort. So we're very lucky." Mayo's partnership model—integrating expertise from a wide variety of sources—helps advance its singular goal of improving patient outcomes.

In other organizational environments, however, workforce participants may have different goals and objectives, sometimes even within the same team. While all participants need to have their interests aligned, they may have distinct individual goals. For instance, a freelance designer may want to not only contribute appropriate and acceptable design work to a project but also build a portfolio to promote an independent design consultancy. The designer may be building skills to use for a different client. In a workforce ecosystem, these mutually beneficial goals—meeting project objectives while explicitly building one's own brand—can reinforce each other, resulting in high-quality work with multiple beneficial outcomes. Leaders need to recognize and embrace these diverse interests, and align opportunities to achieve outcomes valuable to all. In these situations, building an aligned team may be a more realistic goal than building a unified one.

Hybrid teams comprising employees and external contributors, often in different geographic locations, represent another leadership challenge of orchestrating workforce ecosystems. Chamorro-Premuzic, chief innovation officer at ManpowerGroup, observes, "Managing a hybrid workforce is different. We've all experienced this already: you're in a meeting, and eight people are in a room, and then there are four or five people somewhere else. Do you have two meetings? What are the underlying politics?" With external contributors in the mix, in addition to remote employees, it's even more difficult for leaders to gain alignment toward common strategic goals.

Board Leadership and Workforce Ecosystems

Once a workforce ecosystem becomes an essential strategic element for an organization, it enters the purview of the board of directors. Some boards are already beginning to look at workforce ecosystems through the lens of risk and competitiveness. We see boards focused on risks related to workforce ecosystems, such as having an insufficient ability to ramp up and down the skills and capabilities the organization needs (which can be ported from the outside), not conforming to compliance and regulatory standards (including co-employment and data privacy), and incurring damage to the organization's reputation (in regard to, for instance, the treatment of gig workers, or increased automation or reliance on AI). MetLife's board is focused on how the company is advancing its access to skills. Susan Podlogar, executive vice president and chief human resources officer at MetLife, says she hears from directors asking, "Do we have the right skills in the organization? And if not, how are we searching beyond our own boundaries to get access?"

Companies are only "scratching the surface on governance for workforce ecosystems," maintains Wels, former executive vice president of HR at the consumer goods giant Unilever. He sees this changing in the near future:

> I can imagine that pretty soon businesses will have nonexecutive boards to ask questions around, "How are you managing the value chain of your inner and outer workforce or your inner and outer core?" Because if you want to be an attractive company, you want to stay employer of choice and have access to new skills so that the cost to recruit is lower and a competitive advantage. You need to make sure that you actually transform the industry from a quality-of-work perspective as well. So I can imagine the board starting to ask those questions, and then investors are going to ask those questions.

Boards of directors must not only understand the nature of workforce ecosystems and their drivers but also incorporate workforce ecosystem perspectives and appropriate questions into their corporate governance practices.

Organizational Culture and Workforce Ecosystems

In almost every discussion we have with leaders and managers about workforce ecosystems, the concept of organizational culture eventually rises to the surface. In some cases, managers lament the difficulties of integrating external workers into their cultures. They mention legal constraints that prevent them from going too far in treating external workers like employees and note that the short-term nature of many external engagements makes it infeasible to pursue cultural integration. Other managers point out that their experiments with pursuing a single unified culture have not worked. They concluded that some workforce ecosystem engagements are primarily transactional and should remain that way. In some instances, there is no need for a relationship-building element, and participants, either external or internal, or both, really don't want or need highly integrated culture building. Leaders have many choices to make related to building a workforce ecosystem culture. Is their organizational culture only for employees, or a broader set of workers and participants? How should an organizational culture be extended to embrace an extended workforce? Leadership, culture, and workforce ecosystem orchestration go hand in hand.

In 1985, Ed Schein published his now-classic book *Organizational Culture and Leadership*. The opening paragraph of the preface argues that culture and leadership cannot be separated:

> The purpose of this book is, first of all, to clarify the concept of "organizational culture" and, second, to show how the problems of organizational leadership and organizational culture are basically intertwined. I hope to demonstrate that organizational culture helps to explain many organizational phenomena, that culture can aid or hinder organizational effectiveness, and that leadership is the fundamental process by which organizational cultures are formed and changed.[5]

The issues surrounding culture and workforce ecosystems are similarly intertwined. When the organization includes a mix of participants both within and outside the bounds of the formal structure, what challenges does that present for building and managing an organizational culture? Are traditional notions of how to create and retain an organizational culture valid in a workforce ecosystem? How comprehensive and inclusive should the culture be? To what extent should it be consistent across the central organization and through interactions within the ecosystem structure?

This section explores the composition and maintenance of organizational culture in workforce ecosystems. Relevant issues include navigating tensions surrounding inclusion and collaboration among internal and external workers, managing hybrid and heterogeneous cultures, and addressing areas in which relationships are less defined and continuously changing.

Culture in a Workforce Ecosystem: Variability in Approaches

At PlanOmatic, a company providing photos, floor plans, and 3D scans for the real estate industry, CEO Kori Covrigaru reaches out personally to welcome each new contractor to the organization.[6] For PlanOmatic, this community of contractors, called PlanOtechs, is essential to the operation of the business, whose contractors far outnumber its employees. For a time, PlanOmatic sponsored a company-wide program of competitions and icebreaking activities to integrate PlantOtechs into the company's culture. Because there were so many contractors, each team included two employees and three contractors. "It was fun," Covrigaru recalls

> But ultimately it's really hard to get contractors to embrace the culture. Typically contractors will have multiple gigs going on. They are their own brand; they are their own culture. Trying to instill these core values and get buy-in from people who may be here one day a week, two days a week, and trying to figure out where that balance was—there was not a one-size-fits-all solution to bring them in. Also, contractors tend to come and go a lot more than employees do. We sort of fizzled out that program. That was difficult for us.

As PlanOmatic's experience suggests, leaders confront tensions surrounding how comprehensive and homogeneous an enterprise's culture ought to be relative to internal and external contributors. Organizations actively embracing workforce ecosystems are managing these tensions in a range of ways. Their strategies run the gamut from concentrating primarily on organizational culture for internal employees, with little to no focus on culture for external contributors, to managing a hybrid workforce ecosystem culture with defined priorities for employees and a parallel set of distinct priorities for external workers, to aiming to adopt a common cultural portfolio across the workforce ecosystem, encompassing both internal and external members. One way to envision this is to consider a set of culture-related scenarios ranging from employee-centric to homogeneous; below we outline these three scenarios.

Scenario 1: Employee-Centric Culture

Some leaders focus primarily on their employee culture, and are relatively unconcerned with engendering a common culture that includes external gig workers, contractors, and contributing organizations. Ceridian's Tohyama believes that in key product areas, companies should remain centered on ensuring a consistent culture with internal workers. "A product-focused company requires a core team of people who understand everything about that product and how you want to take that product forward," she says. "If you lead a design team, for example, and 50 percent of the team is external, you must ensure the other internal 50 percent of team members are intrinsically embedded in what the company does so that you aren't betraying those core tenets of your product and the culture of your company." Tohyama believes that culture is far less important for external workers. She argues, "If you're getting in someone externally for a short-term project, do they intrinsically have to understand the culture of the company? They have to understand a little bit of it. But we're hiring them for that skill set they have."

Scenario 2: Different Cultures across Workforce Ecosystem

PlanOmatic eventually and somewhat reluctantly abandoned its company-wide team-building activities because external workers weren't interested in participating, and it wasn't clear the activities were providing value to the organization and workforce. It became evident that the company didn't need activities to gain the engagement across the workforce ecosystem. For some groups of external contributors, like international workers, however, the company recognized the need to have some cultural management and alignment. Covrigaru notes that when PlanOmatic works with overseas providers of contractors, the company looks for partners whose values align with PlanOmatic's. "Our culture is really important to our company, but it's hard to convey that overseas," Covrigaru says. "So we work with a partner that shares similar values, and understands that company culture and core values are extremely important to us."

In many organizations, mergers and acquisitions activities often lead to leadership challenges, including managing cultural differences. This is particularly acute in organizations that extensively acquire other companies, like Roche, one of the world's largest biotech and medical solutions companies. In these cases, acquired company employees become part of internal workforces, but their groups frequently continue to act like external entities. The acquired entities are undoubtedly part of workforce ecosystems and raise interesting questions about managing hybrid cultures. Cristina A. Wilbur, chief people officer, says Roche is sensitive to respecting existing cultures at newly acquired companies. She explains, "When we acquire companies, we are very mindful of the things that are most critical to connect into the Roche organization without crushing a culture. If you acquire a company and then you sweep it completely through, you lose the whole sense of why the company was acquired in the first place. Culture is a big part of that."

One company we studied that has been built through extensive acquisitions confronts similar issues with its subsidiaries. Previously, the organization's acquired companies competed with each other, but competition has largely been replaced by cooperation in response to changing customer demand. The company has had to revise its approach to culture in turn. "Our company was built by acquisition," a senior executive explained. "The holding companies were built to be a collection of companies that were good at their specific offerings. For decades they were competing with each other inside the company. Now clients want an integrated solution, so we have a company that used to compete, that's now connected." That shift, the executive says, is better served by a more inclusive corporate culture—one that retains attributes of each individual unit's unique culture. In short, the culture now includes both elements of an integrated culture and the distinct cultural features of its subsidiaries.

The organization is also rethinking how culture is managed with its thousands of freelance and gig workers. "You have this layer of people who don't work here full-time or at least aren't called employees," the executive notes. "Inside each subsidiary you're going to have your own identity, but there's a core that if you're working at our company, you can be assured there are values you'll be participating in, including training around diversity and inclusion."

Scenario 3: Common Culture across Workforce Ecosystem

Other organizations believe in fostering a common culture for the entire workforce ecosystem, including both internal and external workers as well as various subcategories within these groups.

At Mural, a collaboration software and solutions company, a certain baseline of information on the company's values is "required for all team members, whether they are full-time workers or contractors," Estes says, noting that the company discourages an "us versus them mentality" between internal and external contributors. He continues, "Everybody needs to understand how the company runs, the expectations of how you collaborate, how we treat each other, how we work, and how we define success because it goes into our products and the work that we do."

In a very different organization, the US Army, Lieutenant General Ronald P. Clark, Commanding General at US Army Central at Shaw Air Force Base in South Carolina, expresses a similar conviction. His particular ecosystem includes military personnel, civilian personnel, and contractors. "I've got to make sure that we're building an entire team and that it's inclusive of our contract employees because the rules that apply to us apply to them too," he observes. "We can't have people who are not inside the family being treated differently. They're here—somebody brought them to the family reunion."

In this scenario, different cultures may exist and the ecosystem may benefit by bringing them together. In another example from the US Army, Major General Milford H. Beagle Jr., Commanding General in the 10th Mountain Division at Fort Drum in New York, highlights the challenges. His ecosystem contains wide generational diversity, ranging from baby boomers, who appreciate stability, to members of Generation Z, for whom stability is less essential. He says that to address this, "We have to now set a baseline of, 'Where is that common culture?' Our shared belief is the US Army. We trust our mission." A common culture helps advance the Army's overall mission.

Challenges of Managing Organizational Culture in Workforce Ecosystems

The above scenarios represent different approaches to leadership and organizational culture in workforce ecosystems. Workforce ecosystems are often complex and evolving, resulting in culture-related challenges. Below we present a few examples of the challenges that have emerged through our research.

At Roche, it can be a challenge to delineate internal employees and the contingent workforce, affecting both external workers and internal employees. Jane Weinmann, the company's People and Culture (HR) transformation lead and chief of staff to Cris Wilbur, Roche's chief people officer, says, "In some cases, our contingent workers are so embedded in projects, it feels almost as if they are seamlessly part of the team." Referring to internal employees who may ask about the contractors with whom they work, Weinmann continues, "You sometimes get questions like, 'Why don't they get a bonus?' It's managing that kind of culture of wanting to be collaborative and wanting to be similar with the tensions of the associated employment law issues—that starts to get more challenging."

Based in the Netherlands, Randstad is the world's largest HR services provider matching over 2 million people with jobs in 2021 and serving

235,000 clients. Randstad Sourceright's global chief executive officer, Mike Smith, points out that the need to address these cultural issues is driven by customers in addition to employees. Customers expect anyone with whom they interact at an organization to fully represent the brand; they don't distinguish between different employment models. "I, 100 percent, see organizations saying, the contingent workforce is going to be a critical part of our workforce ecosystem for the future. If we treat them like hired help, they're going to act like hired help," he says. "And our customers don't perceive them to be hired help. They perceive them to be a reflection of the brand. As a result, we need to make sure that the contingent workers are having a great experience day-to-day."

Podlogar navigates a difficult middle ground to get external workers to be committed to MetLife despite their limited time working there.

> How do you make sure they connect with your organization's purpose? We're a relationship-based company so you have to look at how you create that affinity and loyalty. You need to have the right inputs which include—alignment with our purpose, clarity of outcomes, trust and support, a quest for learning and alignment to the business and work. With that level of intention you get the outputs you need—the energy for delivering value. It's also about creating an affiliation for that period of time to harness the potential and contribution of the individual.

Decisions related to culture not only must align with strategic and organizational priorities but also must adhere to legal, regulatory, and normative frameworks. This surfaces a set of challenges involving legal and regulatory concerns associated with culture and contingent workers in particular. Across geographies, laws, policies, regulations, and cultural norms vary in terms of how organizations manage external workers. Too much effort to include them in internal activities raises the risk of their being considered de facto employees. We return to this topic again in part III.

Orchestrating workforce ecosystems thus not only requires new leadership approaches but also a greater understanding of how to manage organizational culture in these contexts.

Action Questions

1. How effective are the managers in your organization at leading teams comprising both internal and external participants?

2. To what extent do leaders and managers in your organization need to grapple with leadership challenges related to relinquishing control as they orchestrate a workforce ecosystem?

3. Has your board of directors begun to consider strategic risks connected with workforce ecosystems? Should it?

4. Are there organizational culture considerations that you should be thinking about across your workforce ecosystem?

5. How does your company's organizational culture address not only internal employees but also the range of external contributors, the extended workforce, involved in creating value for your organization?

   • Does it align with one of the three scenarios in this chapter? Is there a different viable scenario?

   • To what degree do your organization's leaders need to balance risk and legal or regulatory concerns with workforce ecosystem culture strategies?

HR doesn't work directly with contractors; it's a different part of the organization. HR focuses only on W-2 employees.

—Kori Covrigaru, PlanOmatic

Temp labor and contract labor generally sit in operations and report there, not through HR in most cases.

—Meredith Wellard, Deutsche Post DHL

Procurement would procure people, but they'd also procure your pencils. And so they'd have this archaic process that treated pencils like people. They were under pressure to get costs down. You didn't have an organization that was dedicated to trying to figure out how to support the business outside of those very narrow lanes.

—anonymous executive

One distinguishing feature of a workforce ecosystems perspective is that it goes beyond considering a contingent workforce alone (long- and short-term contractors or gig workers); it goes beyond strategic alliances, business ecosystems, or supply chains (with mostly contractual relationships between organizations); and it goes beyond the connections among employees. It includes connections and interdependencies throughout the extended workforce. The particular power of the workforce ecosystem approach is that it blends all of these discussions in a meaningful way. These relationships ultimately are about how an organization harnesses all the resources at its disposal to capture and create value for its customers along with other stakeholders.

This type of orchestration approach contrasts with the default, siloed approach to managing interactions in a workforce ecosystem. Contingent workers are the responsibility of procurement, partners and alliances are often handled by strategy, and AI and automation are part of the tech organization (but rarely regarded as part of the broader workforce ecosystem). Meanwhile, HR oversees full- and part-time employees. In this common approach, multiple groups work independently to govern the contributors for which they have a mandate. The default approach is decentralized and uncoordinated.

In short, companies typically have a disconnected approach to managing the full range of contributors in their workforce ecosystems. The functions and business units have separate, distinct mandates and systems for working with various categories of workers. Orchestrating workforce ecosystems requires a different, more integrated approach.

The word *architecture* is generally used to refer to "the complex or carefully designed structure of something."[1] We use the phrase *integration architectures* to discuss how distinct parts of a workforce ecosystem come together in a coordinated way. Integration architectures relate to two main types of relationships in workforce ecosystems. First, they help to codify how functions within an organization, such as HR, procurement, and IT, coordinate among themselves. Second, integration architectures capture how organizations interact with their extended workforce.

Leaders, managers, and ecosystem participants themselves have a strong role to play in bringing together as well as coordinating all the various parts of these extended workforces.

In chapter 3, we identified three key characteristics of workforce ecosystems; *coordination* is one of these Three Cs. Coordination describes the extent to which an organization controls or governs its workforce ecosystem. The idea of integration architectures extends this conversation about coordinating because it reflects *how* an organization becomes coordinated.

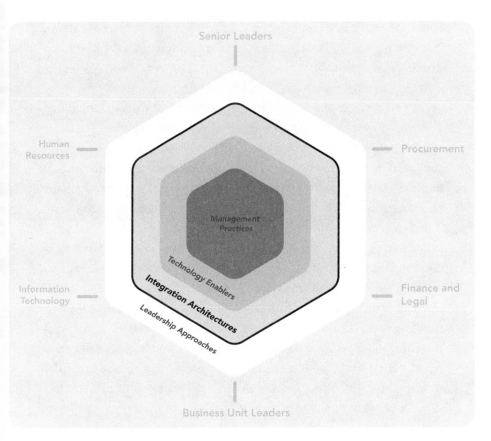

Figure 6.1
Integration architectures in the workforce ecosystem orchestration framework.

Figure 6.1 highlights the second-innermost hexagon in our orchestration framework, which represents integration architectures. In the remainder of this chapter, we explore decentralized and centralized approaches to integration architectures, a phased approach to building these architectures, and the application of integration architectures to relationships with (and among) an extended workforce.

Decentralized Integration Architectures

Managers in different departments with diverse needs frequently use combinations of external and internal workers without any centralized coordination. At one company we studied, the management of external and internal workers was highly fragmented before the COVID-19 pandemic. According to its HR vice president, "HR really only paid close attention to what was going on with the full-time-equivalent employees or part-time employees." Often with contingent workers, she noted, "HR was not in the loop at all." There wasn't even an agreed-on understanding at that time about what was meant by the company's contingent workforce. These decentralized approaches may be efficient on a local level, where each business unit and functional manager retains maximum control. But they are suboptimal at an aggregate level.

Indeed, decentralization can have substantive drawbacks when orchestrating a workforce ecosystem. Dispersed efforts may not be aligned with the overall strategic priorities for the workforce ecosystem and may undermine the pursuit of new strategic directions. The lack of integration may mean a dearth of data about who (and what) is contributing to an organization. It may mean inefficiencies in costs as contingent workers are sourced on an ad hoc basis. And it likely means that both internal workers and external contributors (existing and potential) have less visibility into opportunities to contribute. While decentralization is currently the most common approach to managing employees and the extended workforce, it is almost always uncoordinated.

We recognize that it may be possible to use technology to overcome some of these shortcomings and still maintain a siloed, decentralized approach to orchestrating a workforce ecosystem. For example, the ecosystem can include substantial connectivity and strong relationships among members through the use of digital talent marketplaces and networked data systems that track information about ecosystem participants. Such a system would create a loosely connected yet still essentially decentralized approach to orchestration.

Centralized Integration Architectures

For all the reasons above and more, many organizations orchestrating workforce ecosystems are creating integration architectures that are more centralized and cross-functional in their design. These vary considerably in both scope and tactics, yet all seem to put a great emphasis on collaboration across functional areas. Some organizations are integrating workforce ecosystem management with HR assuming a coordinating role with procurement and technology; in these cases, business leaders and teams work with HR and others as they source as well as manage diverse and expansive workforce teams. Leaders proactively manage risks, and business teams view internal, external, and technological talent as sources of competitive advantage. Other companies are centralizing as well, but adopting a more cross-functionally integrated approach to managing all types of individual workers; in these cases, HR plays a key but less central role. Still other organizations are focusing on centralizing their access to external workers and using technological systems such as talent marketplaces to enable this integration architecture.

Below we provide a few examples of centralized integration architectures in emerging workforce ecosystems.

Swiss global health care company Novartis has set up a cross-functional steering committee to manage its approximately 110,000 internal workers and roughly 50,000 external ones. Markus Graf envisions a more active role for HR in developing what he calls a "holistic view on talent." This holistic approach will entail turning over the management of contingent workers to HR, and collaborating between talent acquisition and talent management as a single function. Novartis is working on providing managers with data-driven visibility into internal and external talent sources culled from a variety of partners and platforms. The process will be facilitated by curators called "workforce strategists," who will grant managers real-time access to teams of employees, contractors, and technologies.

Historically, Roche's management of different worker groups was extremely fragmented. Cristina Wilbur says of the contingent workforce, "People were taking their different pieces, which I think classically happens. There was no one really owning it holistically." The COVID-19 pandemic changed that. The company began manufacturing COVID-19 tests and had to fold in a large number of contractors to meet the exploding demand. Wilbur explains that, during this period of instability, many workers at Roche had a strong desire to not only take care of their own employees, but also their external workforce. "Quite a lot of colleagues said, 'OK, how are we going to deal with the contractors? How about our contingent staff?' It was not just 'I'm looking out for myself,' it was really this sense of unity and solidarity to look across the entire system and say, these are all people contributing to our business continuity during the COVID-19 situation. This sense of care is deeply rooted in our culture and purpose."

To respond to these concerns, Roche's People & Culture function (HR) has taken ownership and defined a holistic global framework for how to manage Roche's external workforce (contractors, contingent workers, consultants, and managed services). The COVID crisis accelerated the need to change the company's long-term approach. As a result, Wilbur says, "We've been thinking about our workforce in a much more inclusive, holistic way." The entire workforce, of both internal and external contributors, is now holistically considered by a group in People & Culture called Integrated Workforce Strategies (IWS), which uses cross-functional collaboration throughout the business to make staffing more seamless and effective.

Roche is also taking a more integrated approach to talent acquisition overall. Wilbur describes the company's system of resources and tools for identifying collaborators across the ecosystem: "IWS helps us to think of our workforce end-to-end," she says. "It looks at the recruitment and acquisition part of bringing people into the organization, from attracting to marketing, internally and externally."

As with Roche, the pandemic prompted HR at another globally distributed company that we studied to get more involved with overseeing the broader workforce amid concerns related to both remote and on-site work policies, pay continuity, absenteeism, and the need for sick leave—issues affecting contingent workers as much as employees. Regarding the contingent workforce, an HR executive explained that management was asking itself, "Who are they? Where are they? Can we find them quickly if we need to? How do we track them down through our suppliers? Are our suppliers prepared to partner with us on retaining these employees?" The pandemic lent urgency to the idea that the company would have to be more centrally integrated and agile to take care of its contingent workers. The pandemic also accelerated existing feelings at the company that it needed to better manage the reputational, legal, operational, and cost risks of the broader workforce, and use the entire workforce to its fullest competitive advantage.

Specific business units sometimes have worked on their own to access resources that they need. At this same company, for instance, hiring practices used to follow different processes and procedures depending on the department—and departments tended not to communicate with one another. HR supported decisions about hiring permanent employees, while procurement brought in contingent workers. Meanwhile, unbeknownst to HR, managers were often converting contingent workers into full-time employees. With a newly developed clearinghouse platform, this company created data-based cross-functional visibility into tracking and approving external workers, involving HR, procurement, and finance.

The chief procurement officer of the company explains the legacy thinking that made the management of the contingent workforce a "hot potato" at the company. "Anybody who was at the center was on the hook for all the risk and none of the benefit." Now, he says, the company is shifting to think of its relationship with this workforce in strategic rather than transactional terms. This strategic approach also involves managing the contingent workforce cross-functionally:

> When you look at it holistically, this actually is a strategic weapon in the arsenal if you're managing it in the right way. It becomes less of a hot potato. That's still an uphill battle because that's not the traditional way of thinking about it. But I don't think you can manage this in a silo. If you try and park it in HR, you try and park it in procurement, you try and park it in legal, you're going to fail. If you don't have a cross-functional body, whether a clearinghouse or something similar, it reverts back into an unmanaged asset.

The HR executive maintains, "There was an acknowledgment between our CFO, our chief general counsel, our CHRO, and our chief operating officer that they all had skin in the game."

Other organizations are realizing the importance of cross-functional coordination and the utilization of data when it comes to talent acquisition. Randstad Sourceright's Mike Smith describes one of the company's large global customers, which has created "a 'workforce of the future' task force made up of cross-functional individuals from HR, procurement, talent acquisition, and business leaders for tax consulting." Smith continues, "It's their job to effectively break down the traditional silos of buying behavior. Typically, HR and talent acquisition would own permanent hiring, procurement would own contingent hiring, IT projects would be done by line of business heads, etc. And what that group is designed to do, is say, 'How do we work together to get a better understanding of leveraging the ecosystem in a more efficient way?'" In this case, the client company is deploying a more integrated architecture to orchestrate its workforce ecosystem.

Talent marketplaces are another great tool for anchoring a centralized and more cross-functionally integrated architecture. NASA is beginning to centralize the integration of its workforce ecosystem by starting with internal resources; it will move later to integrate external contributors by extending the same system. The space agency's digital transformation group uses a talent marketplace to coordinate access to machine talent and internal human talent for gigs and projects. NASA's Nicholas Skytland says that in the past, orchestration of the workforce ecosystem was "pretty fractured." But NASA now has "one orchestrating mechanism" that locates talent. Skytland recalls that

> prior to this, NASA had ten different centers, and each of the centers was doing its own thing when it came to matching internal talent with tasks. We had six different talent marketplace platforms internally at the agency. We brought them all down into one, improved it, and rolled out an agency-wide platform. However, it is not yet integrated to be able to access external talent. When it comes to the gig economy, to project-based workers external to NASA who are not employees, we think about it now from a procurement

standpoint, as a contract. It has to transform, and that's one of the places we hope to innovate within the agency.

All of these examples represent organizations moving to more centralized and cross-functionally integrated architectures. They vary in degree, with some intentionally coordinating only internal employee movements, others focusing only on contractor activities, and still others considering more comprehensive approaches by building cross-functional teams as well as including all types of workers and even technologies.

Building Integration Architectures for Workforce Ecosystems

While centralized and cross-functional integration architectures are enabling organizations to achieve higher levels of coordination in their workforce ecosystems, these efforts are in their nascent stages, only barely beginning to take shape. Even among companies on the leading edge of workforce ecosystem transformations, leaders emphasize that efforts are just starting to gain traction. In our research and consulting, we see that most organizations still use reactive, local, and uncoordinated approaches to enlisting and retaining external talent and complementary contributors.[2]

Leaders realize that such decentralized efforts are both cost and resource inefficient, and risk demotivating internal employees. Yet they struggle to establish a centralized cross-functionally integrated architecture for workforce ecosystem orchestration. We have heard the following concerns:

- How do you identify the right set of stakeholders to create a centrally integrated architecture for workforce ecosystem orchestration?
- How do you get stakeholders to engage in local workforce ecosystem experiments to tailor shared goals to specific contexts?
- How do you promote coordinated learning from local experimentation?
- How do you improve your workforce ecosystem implementation process over time?

Companies are beginning to address these concerns by, for instance, adopting software systems (e.g., SAP Fieldglass) to manage diverse types of external workers in a more integrated way.[3] PayPal engages freelancers in multiple countries with varying labor regulations, and uses a centralized system to manage compliance risk and control costs.[4] Similarly, Europe's largest electronics company, Siemens, engages over six thousand external workers with $150 million in annual spending. While divisions within the organization initially managed these engagements separately, Siemens has moved to an integrated system enabling unified reporting and management.[5] Across industries, we see organizations grappling with the intricacies, costs, and opportunities of workforce ecosystems, and adopting solutions to more holistically orchestrate them.

One solution is for companies to use a phased process to orchestrate more integrated workforce ecosystems in a way that connects decentralized efforts with a centralized approach. This process is likely to be most appropriate for large, established organizations starting to embrace workforce ecosystems, but key elements should be helpful for all types of workforce ecosystems, including those in small and medium enterprises. The process includes identifying challenges and embarking on four phases to address them. These challenges can be categorized as structural (pertaining to the division of labor, goals, and incentives), political (relating to resources, power, and status), and cultural (affecting individuals' search for identity and meaning) (see figure 6.2).[6]

In the first phase, we propose creating an orchestration team at the center to develop a working plan, goals, and metrics for workforce ecosystem orchestration in consultation with relevant local and central stakeholders, both internal and external. This team should focus on integration considerations both within the organization (functional roles and responsibilities) and also relationships with external participants. By working with groups within the organization that already engage external workers, the team can get a head start with managers experienced in orchestrating parts of workforce ecosystems. From a structural design perspective, they can quickly begin to highlight

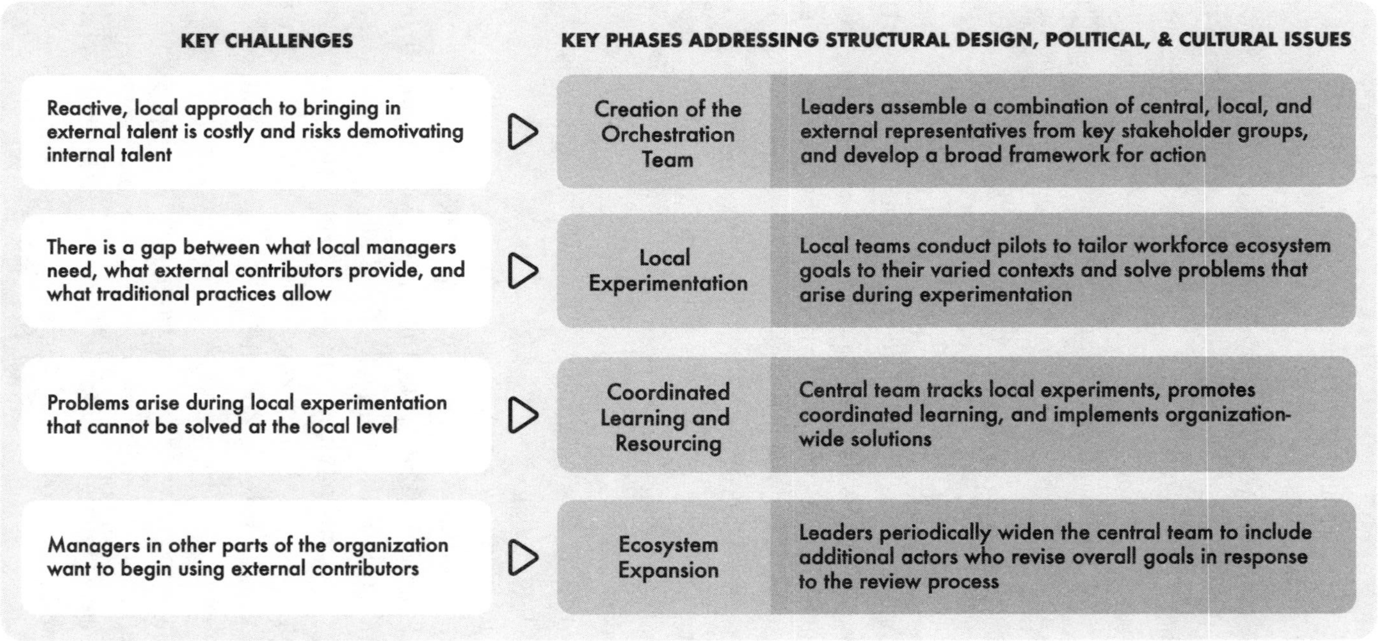

KEY CHALLENGES		KEY PHASES ADDRESSING STRUCTURAL DESIGN, POLITICAL, & CULTURAL ISSUES
Reactive, local approach to bringing in external talent is costly and risks demotivating internal talent	△ Creation of the Orchestration Team	Leaders assemble a combination of central, local, and external representatives from key stakeholder groups, and develop a broad framework for action
There is a gap between what local managers need, what external contributors provide, and what traditional practices allow	△ Local Experimentation	Local teams conduct pilots to tailor workforce ecosystem goals to their varied contexts and solve problems that arise during experimentation
Problems arise during local experimentation that cannot be solved at the local level	△ Coordinated Learning and Resourcing	Central team tracks local experiments, promotes coordinated learning, and implements organization-wide solutions
Managers in other parts of the organization want to begin using external contributors	△ Ecosystem Expansion	Leaders periodically widen the central team to include additional actors who revise overall goals in response to the review process

Figure 6.2

Four phases of orchestrating an integrated workforce ecosystem.

and address previously identified skills gaps. To deal with political concerns, the team can choose local well-respected and action-oriented champions to lead transformations. Additionally, the team can include representatives from external contributors in order to bring their perspectives to the efforts. Team members should be able to speak for functional areas, product groups, and business units as appropriate; the key is to obtain participation from across stakeholder groups. Finally, to grapple with cultural challenges, at least one team member should play the role of a boundary spanner, serving as a go-between among the central team, local teams, and other affected groups.

In the second phase, we suggest promoting local experimentation. Central orchestration teams can introduce pilot programs to explore potential configurations of workforce ecosystem relationships. These experiments can address structural issues such as staffing projects with a mix of internal and external workers, identifying necessary skills, ensuring competencies, and measuring the quality of outcomes. They can address political challenges such as internal employees resisting contributions from external workers and local leaders feeling tension as they lose some control over team composition. Finally, cultural questions may arise as employees adapt to shifts in responsibilities, especially if they need to take more of a facilitation role coordinating participants from various sources.

In the third phase, we emphasize coordinated learning and resourcing, spanning challenges (and successes) identified by local teams and overseen by the central team. In this phase, we look for structural impediments, such as existing policies and procedures (e.g., intellectual property licensing models, training rules, etc.) that may serve the organization well in a traditional employee life cycle model, but require revision for a workforce ecosystem. Resourcing issues may arise as local managers hire more external workers or partner more easily with subcontractors, but then refuse to release employees to accept other opportunities. Culturally, it may be the middle tier of management that is resistant even when the C-suite and lower levels embrace changes related to workforce ecosystems. These managers are the ones tasked with managing the day-to-day challenges of these sometimes highly disruptive transformations.

In the final or fourth phase, we consider workforce ecosystem expansion. Once initial pilots are analyzed and new practices are starting to be institutionalized, leaders should consider what other new systems, tools, goals, metrics, and processes have proven successful enough to adopt. Of course, these should be regularly reviewed as the organization continues to learn more about orchestrating workforce ecosystems. Leaders may want to expand the central orchestration team to include representation from other groups within the organization. They may want to consider connecting their workforce ecosystems with others— for example, working more closely with client organizations and their ecosystems. Culturally, leaders may consider more actively promoting distributed learning and workforce ecosystem activities through storytelling and other communication tools. They will likely want to highlight growth opportunities while also beginning to address the myriad concerns that inevitably accompany such transformations.

In sum, this four-phase approach is a start at understanding and addressing the structural, political, and cultural challenges brought about by orchestrating an integrated workforce ecosystem. This approach, guided by the action questions presented throughout this book, can be a practical way to engage, connect, and activate the various players involved in leading and managing workforce ecosystems. It can set in motion a way for organizations to begin to shape their own strategies and pathways for workforce ecosystem orchestration by experimenting with new types of integration architectures, and quickly iterating as they learn what does and doesn't work across different contexts.

Integrating Architectures and External Contributors

In the previous section, our focus was primarily on integration among functional groups within an organization as they grapple with challenges of orchestrating workforce ecosystems. Another component of integration architectures is how an organization manages relationships with its extended workforce. These contributors perform work for the enterprise, but may or may not be contractually engaged by the organization. They play a critical role in creating value for customers and essentially work on behalf of an organization, but their relationship to the organization may take many different forms. Some have extensive contractual relationships and may supply exclusively to the organization; others may not have a contractual relationship at all, but provide an accessory product or service that makes the organization's product much more functional.

By way of example, video game console manufacturers often enable third-party developers (complementors) to create games that work on their systems; frequently, it is the demand for these third-party games that drives sales of particular consoles.[7] Bringing these third-party entities into the company's workforce ecosystem and determining the most appropriate way to manage these relationships could be critical to improving business outcomes. To what extent the games should be tested for compatibility, and whether this should be done by the console manufacturer, a third party, or a crowdsourced community, are all essential decisions that fall under the discussion of integration architectures and workforce ecosystem orchestration. A business development or ecosystem management organization may play the point role in managing these relationships, but needs to coordinate with other functions across the organization. This provides another illustration of how orchestrating a workforce ecosystem requires organizations to think more broadly, and often strategically, about whom they are engaging with and how they need to manage these integrations.

Action Questions:

1. Is your organization best served with a decentralized integration architecture that keeps most orchestration of the workforce ecosystem siloed in various groups?

2. Does someone (or some group) need to be centrally responsible for overseeing the entire workforce ecosystem? If so, who (or what group)? And how? What might a centralized integration architecture look like in your workforce ecosystem?

3. Relative to relationships between internal and external ecosystem members, how stringent will requirements be on participants in the ecosystem, particularly those that operate at arm's length, such as app developers (complementors)?

7 Technology Enablers

Technology plays a key role in orchestrating workforce ecosystems. Technologies enhance and enable capabilities for managing workforces that operate across and beyond organizational boundaries. They can also facilitate new relationships along with novel ways of collecting and analyzing data relevant to workforce ecosystems. For example, by utilizing sophisticated algorithms and data processing, digital talent marketplaces provide workers with access to meaningful work and other opportunities, while at the same time offering managers more ways to source new capabilities and skills.

In our workforce ecosystem orchestration framework introduced in chapter 4, technology enablers are represented in the third-innermost hexagon (see figure 7.1). This hexagon encompasses five types of technologies, all of which we explore in this chapter: *work tech, workforce tech, workplace tech, credentialization and verification tech*, and *technology as participant in workforce ecosystems*. Notably, these technologies encompass far more than legacy HR systems like those you would find in an HR technology stack focused on employee management and interactions. This group of technologies constitutes a broader, richer, and more varied set of systems and tools compared to those traditionally found within an HR function. The demands of orchestrating workforce ecosystems call for a new portfolio of technology enablers.

Companies are wrestling with how to develop, implement, and most effectively leverage individual technologies in these categories. Even more, they are grappling with how to use the technologies together,

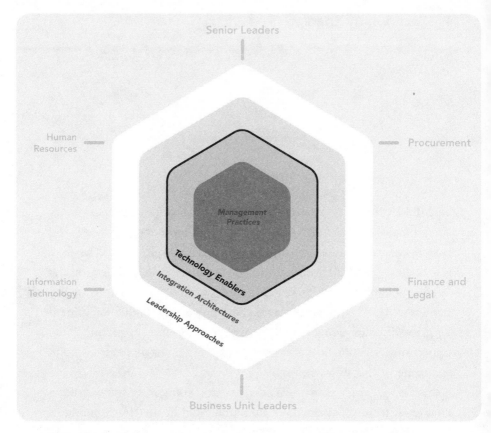

Figure 7.1
Technology enablers in the workforce ecosystem orchestration framework.

sometimes through sophisticated integrations. They are aiming to address new challenges posed by workforce ecosystem orchestration, such as enabling managers to determine which types of resources to access in specific circumstances and then helping to engage them. Initial explorations show that some issues cut across all of these technology categories, including data strategy and technology-driven organizational change. Some decisions about how to address these challenges will partly depend on an organization's workforce ecosystem, the state of an organization's existing technology infrastructure, and how well functions work together. These are early days even for the most advanced leaders of workforce ecosystems.

Work Tech

Technologies from spreadsheets to robots to algorithms are enhancing the productivity and augmenting the capabilities of the workforce.[1] Work tech is the category of tools and technologies we use to help us do our work—everything from bots to medical diagnostic tools to navigation tools. In the health care industry, for example, AI is helping radiologists, surgeons, and physicians improve outcomes as well as reduce costs. In the fall of 2020, Goldman Sachs issued a series of reports and podcasts on the future of work and the growth of a new era of productivity software. Heather Bellini and Ryan Nolan explore the "opportunity for software to unlock productivity gains in the world's 1.25 billion knowledge workers."[2] As combinations of people and technology become increasingly responsible for work in the enterprise, work tech influences both the composition of workforce ecosystems and how to orchestrate them.

Thomas W. Malone, director of the Center for Collective Intelligence at MIT's Sloan School of Management, offers a useful perspective on how technology can help people work together to create *superminds*, which he defines as "a group of individuals acting together in ways that seem intelligent." Malone points out that technology now has the potential to contribute to the intellectual as well as physical activities of these groups. In his perspective, a good way to view work tech is to move from thinking about putting humans in the loop to putting computers in the group. That means, as Malone puts it, "Computers use their specialized intelligence to tackle parts of the problem, people use their general intelligence to do the rest, and computers help coordinate larger groups of people than has ever been possible."[3] The evolution of technology is likely to influence the nature and role of superminds across workforce ecosystems.

Workforce Tech

This category includes those technologies related to managing employees; they are typically used by the HR function. While these technologies have been updated and extended during the past decade to operate on mobile devices and run on the cloud, they still remain decidedly centered on employee management. But a growing number of companies are seeking more comprehensive technology systems to provide total workforce management, covering both internal and external workers.

Markus Graf at Novartis offers a case in point. The pharmaceutical company is integrating a portfolio of workforce tech systems to create a total workforce management platform. With a workforce of 160,000 (approximately 110,000 employees along with 50,000 external workers and contractors), Novartis is creating an integrated workforce management system that brings together a range of technologies including HR systems, talent marketplaces, and learning platforms. At Novartis, this involves working toward what Graf calls a "talent skills ecosystem to access specific skills through building a common language, and making sure the technologies that we use talk with each other to create a seamless experience and flow of data across the portfolio of different workforce technologies." He adds,

> Right now, most of the information related to contractors is in SAP Fieldglass, which is mainly a procurement platform, but co-owned by and codeveloped with HR. As you want to manage workforce more intentionally and externally as well, the HR team will play a more active role. We see more joint responsibility between talent management and the talent acquisition organization. While it's currently not yet one unit, the vision is to get there as we start to embrace this integrated workforce strategy. It's becoming elevated as a priority within the organization.

Pulling Together Disparate Systems to Enable Workforce Ecosystems
A key moment in our research arose when Graf summarized his organization's thinking. He explained how Novartis is working to have its systems integrated so that managers can find and access the appropriate resources at the appropriate time. Essentially, the vision that Graf and Novartis are putting forth represents exactly the form of technology enabler that will allow leaders and managers to have one consolidated way to find the right resources from across a workforce ecosystem. He says,

Our vision is pretty simple. We want to see something that plugs into Microsoft Teams, our collaboration technology. As managers create new teams or new projects, they have a button to create a new body of work or activity. And they come to a simple landing page with different workforce resources, internal and external. They may specify a given business need that needs to be completed and the skill sets required to do this work. Then they are guided toward what are the possible and best levers to resource this work.

Building a single integrated technology system that can support sourcing, assessing, placing, managing, and developing talent and skills can be a significant challenge, observes ManpowerGroup's Tomas Chamorro-Premuzic. "None of the smaller, newer, fancy tech firms do even half of these things," he says. The larger tech providers, such as Oracle and SAP, are working to develop their own comprehensive offerings.

In short, workforce tech has evolved. In the past, its primary concern was keeping track of who the employees were, how the firm was paying them, and whether the company was filing the required regulatory reports. Now it enables managers to access skills and capabilities in the form of jobs, gigs, teams, and services; it allows workers to find and take advantage of opportunities to take on jobs, gigs, projects, learning opportunities, and experiences to grow their skills as well as further their careers. These changes are a result of shifts in both scale and scope for workforce tech. In terms of scale, workforce tech is moving from being entirely internal and employee focused to including access to external resources, such as contractors and professional services firms. With respect to scope, workforce tech is similarly expanding as it moves from encompassing systems optimized for transactions, reporting, and compliance, to embracing ones that also address growth, new experiences, and development. Figure 7.2 provides a graphic representation of these shifts.

The figure depicts four segments that classify workforce tech systems and represents how they are becoming more closely integrated. These segments are as follows.

Internal HR and human capital management (HCM) systems manage employee records, transactions, and reporting, including hiring

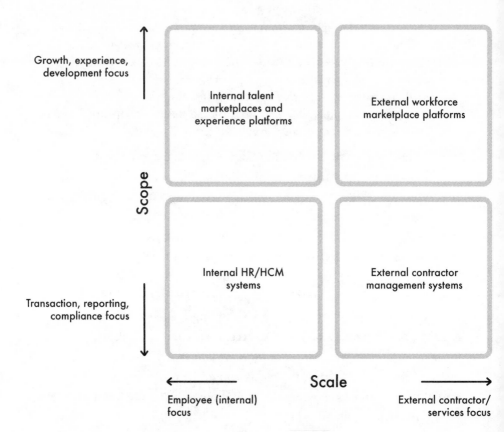

Figure 7.2
Workforce tech: expanding in scope and scale.

records, payroll, and reporting requirements. With other enterprise resource planning (ERP) platforms, these systems have expanded to allow mobile access and cloud-based implementations. Examples include SAP SuccessFactors, Workday, and Oracle Cloud Human Capital Management.

External contractor management systems are managed by procurement to identify, manage, and pay external contractors. Examples include SAP Fieldglass, Beeline, and VNDLY (acquired by Workday in 2021).

Internal talent marketplaces and experience platforms center on workforce experiences, mobility, and growth within and across an enterprise, integrating access to jobs, projects, gigs, learning, development, mentoring, and networking. Their intention is to foster employee choice while providing business managers with increased visibility and access to skills, capabilities, and interests across the organization. Examples include Gloat, Fuel50, Eightfold AI, and new offerings being added by ERP and HCM providers.[4]

External workforce marketplace platforms are a prominent and fast-growing part of workforce tech. They include the online platforms aggregating and connecting workers for freelance, gig, and project work. These platforms can cover a range of skills, or be targeted to specific industries and functions. Examples include Toptal, Fiverr, Upwork, Catalant, Experfy, TaskRabbit, and A.Team.

Workplace Tech

Since the onset of the COVID-19 pandemic, we have experienced the power of technologies that enable virtual and remote work. These include tech to drive distributed work (e.g., Zoom, Microsoft Teams, and WebEx by Cisco); digital reality, including virtual and augmented reality (e.g., Microsoft's HoloLens series); and the metaverse itself, which encompasses 3D virtual worlds that are often connected with each other. Workplace tech is also redesigning physical workspaces to focus on supporting activities that require more intense levels of collaboration. These include designing, creating, learning, and team building, often in hybrid teams of contributors who might be physically present or participating virtually. All of these technologies can enhance the orchestration of workforce ecosystems.

The pandemic intensified the need for workplace technologies. In the spring of 2020 in the United States, the percentage of workforce participants working remotely more than tripled, going from 15 to 50 percent in a matter of weeks.[5] We saw a similar transformation in telemedicine, with clinics reporting a tenfold increase from 2019 to 2020.[6] Chamorro-Premuzic of ManpowerGroup summarizes the mixed response relative to the recent move to remote and virtual work.

"What's very interesting is that we had the technologies and tools to let everyone work from anywhere ten years ago, but there's a reason we didn't do it," he notes. "On the one hand, now we are forced to do it because people experienced it, and we've seen that they're at least as productive, if not more, than before, and in many ways happier and more engaged. On the other hand, people hate change, especially when they're forced to do it." In other words, the challenges associated with the widespread adoption of workplace tech hinge as much on organizational and cultural barriers as on technological ones, echoing the challenges related to the broader adoption and orchestration of workforce ecosystems.

Finally, workplace tech, and the growing prevalence of remote and distributed work, raises some fundamental questions. Diane Gherson, former senior vice president and chief HR officer at IBM, and now a senior lecturer at Harvard Business School, poses probing questions related to contractors and employees who both are doing remote work. "As more and more employees choose to work remotely, and choose not to come into an office and belong to a community, I think there's going to be a question around really what's the difference, right? What's the difference between somebody who's a contractor who only joins us by video, and somebody who is an employee who only joins us by video? And I think that will start to become a bigger issue." This question highlights some of the emerging debates fueled in large part by workplace tech, which not only enables more employees to move into remote roles but also allows organizations to more efficiently engage with increasingly more workforce ecosystem participants of all types as well as from all locations.

Credentialization and Verification Tech

Workers today are earning a range of digital certificates, badges, and tokens along with all manner of new types of credentials. Of course, they are also continuing to receive diplomas from public and private high schools, vocational tech schools, community colleges, universities, and so on. Most who indicate on their résumés and online profiles that they have earned these credentials have in fact done so. Unfortunately, some have not. Moreover, there is no standardization for many of the new credentials. As a case in point, a digital certificate can mean that a participant merely registered and logged in to a seminar for a short period of time, or that the person took and successfully completed multiple college or graduate-level for-credit courses. Most of these new credentials do not have accreditation bodies monitoring them. Even credentials that are genuinely valuable and properly earned may be based on skills that quickly diminish in value as technologies evolve, and yet even the newest credentials, if they are static, do not capture and reflect any diminishment in value over time.

In this world of myriad credentials and experiences, with workers moving more quickly from role to role, a new category of workforce ecosystem technology is evolving encompassing credentialization and verification tech. This technology aims to verify, in real time if possible, applicants' claimed credentials. Developers are creating systems to track the diminishing (or increasing) value of credentials too—for example, dynamic NFTs that can be set to decrease or increase in value over time based on the extent that their holder continues to invest in them (e.g., via taking more classes or gathering new experiences to earn increased value for their credentials). These challenges and opportunities have given rise to the emergence of new technologies, systems, and tools to verify as well as keep track of credentials and experiences, increasingly by using blockchains and related technologies.

The verification of credentials has a long history, dating back to the first résumé, which researchers attribute to the great Renaissance artist and inventor Leonardo da Vinci.[7] In 1482, at the age of thirty da Vinci wrote to the regent of Milan listing eleven things he could do for the city. The list represented his skills, experiences, capabilities, and aspirations. But of course, there was no way to verify any of it. Some credit da Vinci not only with writing the world's first résumé but also with being the first person to overstate his qualifications in writing. Thus was born the now five-hundred-year-old challenge of verifying an applicant's skills and experiences.

One of the global leaders in this emerging field is Dror Gurevich, founder and CEO of the Velocity Network Foundation. According to its website, Velocity Network Foundation is "[reinventing] how career records are shared across the global market. Empowering individuals, businesses and educational institutions through transformational blockchain technology - public, open, trusted and self-sovereign."[8] Gurevich summarizes the problem that Velocity aims to solve: "There are one billion people, roughly, that move jobs every year. They either move between employers or they move within their organization." Someone has to verify that these people are who they say they are, and that they hold the credentials, licenses, employment history, and education that they claim. "There is no easy way to do this today as it requires procuring data from siloed sources. Verification is a significant issue in global markets where 70 percent of employers use third parties to verify credentials," says Gurevich, who adds, "That adds unimaginable cost and friction to the labor market."

He offers the following example:

> Consider that mythical programmer in Serbia who is a third of the price of a Silicon Valley programmer. No one finds this individual because there's not enough data to trust that this person is who they say they are. That's the huge elephant in the room. The Velocity Network Foundation is bringing together leading vendors and solutions providers to build a data utility layer to underlay the global labor market and enable a frictionless experience for individuals and organizations to exchange trusted career and identity credentials.

Regional solutions are being developed and tested as well; for instance, iDatafy's SmartResume® project in Arkansas is working on a "certified résumé" that it is branding with the tagline "A Resume You Can Trust™," which addresses the issue head-on. Mary Lacity, Walton professor of information systems and director of the Blockchain Center of Excellence at the University of Arkansas, describes a regional effort to build a verifiable shared credential network across the state:

> You go to hire somebody. You get their résumé, and now you have a pending three-week investigation. And what do you do? You start calling the issuers: Do they really have a diploma from here? You do a background check with an FBI agent. And the costs add up. One company reported it costs forty thousand dollars per employee for onboarding costs and a lot of it had to do with verification. So if we get this model right, then our talent pool will have a lot less friction in it.

The next phase will scale the SmartResume nationally. In February 2022, iDatafy partnered with the National Student Clearinghouse to load its Comprehensive Learner Records from the Clearinghouse's Myhub digital wallet onto the SmartResume platform. Millions of students will be able to activate a SmartResume on demand through Myhub.

In the frictionless model that Lacity advocates, applicants hold their own digital credentials. "You don't have to go through a LinkedIn," she says.

> You don't have to go through an Indeed. You don't have to call the University of Arkansas to ask if this person got a degree because the proof will be in the person's wallet. Issuers have to buy into the standards we're developing. They issue a digital credential. The public key of the issuer, the only thing that goes on a public blockchain, is proof that that issuer signed the credential. The credential is actually given peer-to-peer to the holder. The verifier has to ask for a peer-to-peer connection. And then the holder says, "OK, you can see where I graduated. You can see I have an SAP certificate."

Streamlining this process can have important benefits beyond reducing verification costs. Lacity gives the example of an award-winning app that the National Health Service in the United Kingdom developed to share credentials to quickly redeploy doctors and nurses across hospitals during the COVID-19 pandemic, and improve both mobility and verification. "It could take from five hours up to a couple of days before the doctor could start working because the new hospital had to verify all the person's qualifications," she says. "Self-sovereign identity is peer-to-peer: the doctor walks in and has all of his or her medical credentials on a smartphone. That new hospital can immediately trust and verify the credentials, and the person goes to work right away."

Technology as Participant in Workforce Ecosystems

We've covered technology's role in workforce, work, workplace, and credentialization systems. Technology can also have a role as a participant in the workforce. In our research over the past several years, this has raised surprising and, for some, unsettling questions.

NASA's Nicholas Skytland captures the issue perfectly, asking,

> What is an employee anymore? The way I boil it down at NASA is technically if you are an employee, it means you have an ID in the NASA IT system. You get a computer, you get an email address, you get a VPN [virtual private network] token, and all of those things. What if an employee might be a bot? None of this is revolutionary. It's just more a matter of, How does an organization actually embrace it and implement that in their organization? That's what we're trying to figure out today. NASA has bots that we consider employees. They're issued badges technically. Essentially, they have an ID in the system because if they didn't, they couldn't even integrate with our IT systems. For a bot to do its basic core function, it has to integrate with our IT systems. We had to make it an employee.

Machines can act as employees when they work alongside human workers, sharing and in some cases doing similar work. Examples include an AI program automatically evaluating insurance claims or parts of jobs being assigned to robotic process automation (RPA) bots. Although for some this is an alarming idea, technology can take on managerial roles as well: a traffic light replaces a traffic officer to direct cars and trucks, or an algorithm matches drivers to requests for rides and replaces a taxi dispatcher.[9] Scheduling software increasingly assigns shifts to employees—a role traditionally performed by humans.

We've seen that technologies play five key roles in orchestrating workforce ecosystems. In table 7.1, we summarize these roles.

Two topics span all five of the roles of technology in orchestrating workforce ecosystems: data strategy and organizational change with

Table 7.1

Summary of technology enablers for workforce ecosystems

Technology Enabler	Description and Roles in Workforce Ecosystems
Work tech	Work tech includes technologies serving as productivity, augmentation, and collaboration tools. These are *technologies we use to do our work* (e.g., spreadsheets, medical diagnostic tools, navigation tools, etc.). Work tech changes what work is done by people, by machines, and by people and machines together.
Workforce tech	Workforce tech includes systems that help organizations manage workforces and help workers access opportunities. It is expanding in two directions beyond traditional HR systems to include internal *and* external workers, and to extend the focus to include workforce dynamics such as mobility, skills, capability access, growth opportunities, new experiences, development, mentoring, and networking.
Workplace tech	Popularized during the first year of the COVID-19 pandemic and continuing to accelerate, workplace tech encompasses technologies that disrupt physical work, and make virtual and remote work possible. Workplace tech is enabling the redesign of physical workspaces to concentrate on activities requiring more intense levels of collaboration, including designing, creating, learning, and team building.
Credentialization and verification technology	Credentialization tech refers to technologies associated with issuing, storing, sharing, and verifying credentials. As workers move more quickly within and across companies, keeping track of credentials—degrees, certificates, badges, and employment and experience history—is essential. The data must be verifiable in real time. Credentialization tech includes network and system strategies, often based on blockchains, to create distributed, fast, and reliable verification.
Technology as participant in a workforce ecosystem	Technology as participant in a workforce ecosystem includes technologies becoming *participants* in workforce ecosystems. As companies issue software licenses for robotic process automation bots and design digital full-time equivalents (FTEs) to off-load work from humans, technology is moving beyond being an enabler of the workforce and facilitator of work; it is becoming part of the workforce itself.

technology enablers. In the following sections we delve into both of these areas.

Data Strategy

As technologies enable new ways to orchestrate workforce ecosystems, we see an accompanying increase in the importance and relevance of data strategy. For example, with platform businesses, which are integral to work and workforce tech, subjects such as data privacy, collection, storage, sharing, access, and monetization, among others, are hot topics for executives, researchers, and the general public.[10] Data-related topics span all the technology categories that we highlighted above, and affect not only the organizations managing systems but also workers, partner companies, and customers.

Using a series of questions, Graf of Novartis underscores the importance of data in orchestrating a workforce ecosystem:

> For large companies, it's a data game, right? What is the data and technology infrastructure that provides you transparency and an understanding of where you are, and empowers you to make more intentional decisions? You can start off with getting data on how many external workers you have. In which part of the organizations do you see them? What is the overall cost of the external workforce? And how do you then make more informed decisions about when to go internal and external, and the like?

MetLife's Susan Podlogar summarizes the data challenge this way in describing the evolution of their talent marketplace and workforce ecosystem strategy,

> We're a data-driven organization. We've been able to analyze data in terms of unlocking discretionary hours from participants. Now we are taking the next click into the data; we're looking at people who've participated in the talent and career marketplaces to see if there is a way to assess their levels of engagement, their retention in the organization, and so on. We made great strides in telling the qualitative data story; now with the data, we are able to add the quantitative impact as well. Our next phase is to conduct longitudinal analytics.

Randstad Sourceright's Mike Smith adds the perspective that we need to view data and systems for all elements of a workforce ecosystem, and keep data up-to-date to ensure it remains valuable to employees, workers, and the company. Smith provides an example of how data can quickly become stale and diminish in usefulness:

> I think what we are seeing is a movement with organizations saying, "We are going to take all the data from these systems, and we're going to keep it up-to-date," because you've got the millions of applicants you've accepted over the years, and as time goes by, their data is not up-to-date. You can't reach out to them for an assignment and say, "Hey, come back and work for us again," because if you don't have their details correct in the system, you're reaching out to someone for a job they're no longer interested in.

Essentially, organizations are recognizing the need to keep their data fresh, and starting to consider how to accomplish that such that the information they have remains relevant and actionable. Related to workforce tech, they should be asking questions like the following:

- To what extent can we interface with external systems such as LinkedIn to cross-check data on the people in our systems?
- How often should we contact individuals asking them to update their data?
- Leveraging verification systems, how can we allow people to self-verify and keep their profiles updated?

Maintaining real-time data and information is one of the core challenges across categories, and especially distinguishes more modern workforce tech from more traditional HR tech. Workforce tech today is increasingly based on marketplace and AI platforms, which are like e-commerce platforms built on interactions and flows. Older HR tech systems have databases and reporting structures as their foundations, yet those don't support the needs of orchestrating today's more interconnected and interdependent workforce ecosystems. A surprising number of executives we interviewed remarked that the most up-to-date information they find about their own employees is not in their own HR systems but rather in publicly available external platforms like LinkedIn. Harnessing marketplace dynamics and AI for internal employee talent and career marketplaces creates new incentives for employees to keep their information and interests up-to-date as well as for business managers to regularly update requirements for available jobs and projects. In sum, data strategy and management challenges span technology categories, and are emerging as an essential focus area for successful workforce ecosystem orchestration.

Technology-Driven Organizational Change

Technology enablers in workforce ecosystems present many of the same organizational change challenges we see whenever dramatic shifts occur in workplaces, especially when they are associated with new technologies. As technology is deployed with almost every employee and team, and marketplace and AI technologies enhance internal marketplaces and work-related systems, the implementation challenges are managerial, organizational, and cultural, as well as technological. It takes time and managerial focus to transform traditional roles, particularly when technology is involved—such as when replacing staffing resource managers with talent marketplaces or shift schedulers with automated scheduling software. The adoption of technologies for orchestrating workforce ecosystems is as much a managerial and organizational challenge as it is a technological one.

Meredith Wellard spoke with us about the intersection of technological adoption and cultural change in the context of workforce ecosystems at Deutsche Post DHL Group. While it is essential that we understand technology trends and discuss their applications, Wellard's account demonstrates that technology deployment conversations go hand in hand with organizational and cultural considerations. She explains the issues that her organization faced related to moving people into new opportunities:

> We have five big divisions plus the central business units. We have every country in the world, and we have everything from our own innovation centers through to traditional finance and HR. What we've noticed is that

people have been limited, and unable to move either out of a function or out of a country or out of a division. They've lacked access either through transparency or because of a talent hoarding mindset of the leader.

Deutsche Post DHL Group (DPDHL Group) decided to try a new approach by leveraging new technologies, and switching its mindset away from functional streams and toward skills that people have and skills that leaders need for projects. Wellard continues by explaining the initial implementations, and underscoring the links between technology and organizational change:

> In early 2020, we did proof-of-concept trials with three different vendors, which was really interesting. We learned a lot about the AI capabilities, about what we mean when we talk about skills. Later in 2020, we formally started the project, got the business case approved, and kicked it off. For me, this is an upside-down project. It's not a technical implementation at all. This is about cultural shift.

DPDHL Group's example highlights how organizations are experimenting with new technologies that enable them to build and manage workforce ecosystems, and require them to consider the organizational consequences of these implementations along the way.

In sum, technology of various sorts plays multiple and diverse roles in orchestrating workforce ecosystems. An effective management approach requires a new understanding of how technology intersects with workforce ecosystems, and a recognition and understanding of the challenges and opportunities associated with data strategy and tech-driven organizational change.

Action Questions

1. Are there specific technologies your organization should be pursuing to enable, improve, and support workforce ecosystem orchestration?
2. Does your organization have an integrated framework for workforce ecosystem technologies that covers and connects the five technology categories outlined above?

3. Does your organization's workforce ecosystem technology framework address the entire workforce ecosystem, including employees, external workforce participants, subcontractors, and complementors?

4. Is your organization's leadership team organized to orchestrate the portfolio of technologies involved with workforce ecosystem orchestration?

5. Should members of your organization's leadership team be actively participating in industry and public policy forums to influence and develop shared technological services related to workforce ecosystems, possibly including standards development, data sharing, and credential verification approaches?

8 Accessing Workforce Ecosystem Members

In the previous chapters, we covered new leadership approaches, integration architectures, and technology enablers, all of which are essential to workforce ecosystem orchestration and depicted in our framework. In chapters 8–9, we delve more deeply into some of the management practices most affected by workforce ecosystems. These practices are represented in our workforce ecosystem orchestration framework illustration by the centermost hexagon (see figure 8.1).

The shift from an employee-based workforce to a workforce ecosystem encompassing employees, individual contract workers, third parties, service providers, contractors, and others has profound implications for workforce management practices. Some executives are keenly aware of the challenges. Jacqui Canney of ServiceNow declares that "the ability to shift management practices for the greater workforce ecosystem is going to be a hard nut to crack." Jeroen Wels, formerly of Unilever, calls managing the external workforce along with the internal workforce "one of the big holy grails to drive productivity for growth in the future." What makes this shift so daunting that an executive reaches for a medieval metaphor to describe the challenge?

A key stumbling block is the widely accepted HR-centric employee life cycle model, which aims to "attract, develop, and retain" employees. This model was well suited to the last century, when organizations would recruit full-time employees, train them, and try to hold onto those who proved most valuable. Workers generally accepted, and often welcomed, a stable, long-term, consistent engagement with an

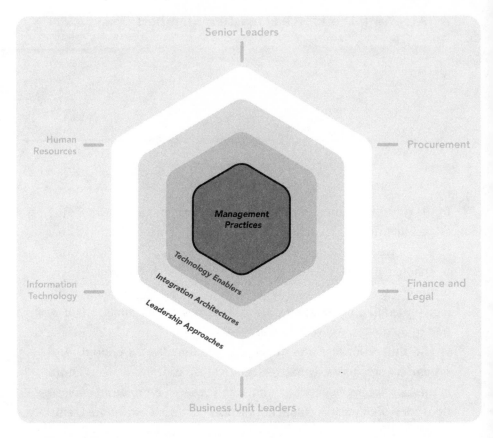

Figure 8.1
Management practices in the workforce ecosystem orchestration framework.

organization and a structured career path that usually provided non-monetary benefits.

The extent to which this increasingly dated model is ingrained in corporate life is difficult to overstate. The HR function is organized around this model, and corporate leadership along with the rest of the functional areas largely accept it. Leaders operate with the underlying assumption that employee-related matters are determined and managed by HR, and that those matters encompass the vast majority of worker—and more broadly, contributor—considerations. Similarly, employee expectations, loyalty, and engagement are determined in no small way by the employee life cycle model, which after all, promises development and promotion opportunities, benefits, retirement packages, and more.

This employee life cycle model is, however, much less useful today—for both organizations and workers—as the types of contributors, from employees to contractors to third-party partners to complementors, have expanded. Workers have longer as well as more varied lives and careers, with various educational and life experience paths. They may be in a marriage or domestic partnership that provides them benefits via a spouse or partner. They may live in a country where the population is entitled to health benefits, such as through the United Kingdom's National Health Service. Or they may desire the flexibility of working for multiple organizations on varied projects, and be willing to manage their own health and retirement benefits. As work today is more dynamic and often project based, with changing skill requirements, it is increasingly performed by external contributors and technologies. NASA's Nicholas Skytland says that focusing on full-time employees is "completely the wrong question." He adds, "What we need to ask is, How do people contribute to advancing the NASA mission? There are many different ways to participate in that, and oh, by the way, you don't have to be human. NASA has bots that we consider employees."

Moving away from the employee life cycle model means changing many of the management practices anchored to it. It means altering how companies attract, develop, and retain (or aim not to retain in some cases) employees and other contributors. It invites more flexibility around who can—and should—do work and for how long, via what means. It requires that companies become more innovative in how they provide employees access to opportunities, and even more forward-thinking in how they address the world of external contributors. It demands a new model, or overall governance structure, that blends external contributors, with their distinctive needs and preferences, and employees, with their distinctive expectations and desires. Finally, it requires that all of this be done in a manner consistent with highly variable national and local laws, policies, and societal expectations.

The scale and scope of these changes for HR, other functional areas, and management more broadly may be daunting. Challenges appear at the policy as well as the day-to-day tactical levels, thereby requiring revised operational decision-making and trade-offs in the context of workforce ecosystems. In this and the following chapter, we break down how specific management practices are likely to change (and in some cases, already are changing) as managers orchestrate workforce ecosystems. We focus on accessing members of the workforce ecosystem, and developing growth opportunities and aligning interests across workforce ecosystems. To help leaders grapple with these shifts, we distill the critical questions that companies need to address to successfully orchestrate an effective workforce ecosystem.

Attracting Many Types of Contributors: Revising Workforce Planning

A more expansive perspective on *who* does work, and *how*, *when*, and *where* work is done, has numerous implications for workforce planning. Mike Smith of Randstad Sourceright observes that organizations are recognizing that the "old sacred cow" of workforce planning, centered on the notion of permanent full-time equivalents (or FTEs), is becoming obsolete. He suggests that workforce planning can no longer be conceived of as a hierarchical process driven entirely by an employer's objectives and requirements; workers' own needs and desires are also driving the transition to a more decentralized yet integrated planning process emphasizing skills and tasks. These worker preferences can also affect organizational strategic decision-making.

We spoke with many executives exploring new employment and engagement models. Without exception, they have moved away from a planning mindset solely revolving around employee acquisition toward an approach centered on gaining access to skills. This shift involves rethinking how they offer opportunities to internal employees and engage with contingent workers. Susan Tohyama describes the evolution in this type of reasoning at Ceridian. She observes, "Early in the pandemic, we focused on growing the skill sets of our people, instead of hiring new external talent. While we're actively hiring externally now, we continue to look to our internal talent marketplace. It's forced employers to think, 'Who do we have? Where are our resources? What skill sets do we really need?" This attitude maintains a high level of attention to internal employee development and movement by expanding the possibilities for employees across the organization; in essence, it is an example of treating employees more like members of an interconnected ecosystem.

At Novartis, executives have an ambitious goal for workforce planning that's targeted to skills. Markus Graf explains,

> Our vision is to have a tool for managers so as people create new teams or projects, they have a button that says, "Create new body of work." Then they land on visualizations of what can be resourced, internally or externally, based on required skill sets. Dashboards, based on ten to eleven different data providers, will enable managers to fully understand how their workload is set up now, and possibilities for further optimization and accessing specific talent pools. The manager will continue to be empowered in our culture, and will gather data on availability and skills costs to inform decision-making. Our skills-based workforce planning projects provide data to managers based on things like current workforce segmentation, internal-external cost, availability, cost trends, and the like. One of the key pillars in our talent strategy is talent intelligence: leveraging data on skills we need in the future, and how to build, buy, and borrow them.

Organizations also are recognizing that they need to adjust to new worker preferences about not only when and where they work but also *how* they relate to their employer. Unilever plans to offer workers more choice in this regard, as Wels explains:

> Unilever is going to explore how you can get to new and modern employment models and contracts. It could be that you are a young father who wants to spend more time with your kids, but you want to prepare yourself during that period for new skills. You can come and say, "I want to work for 30, 40, 50 percent"—whatever the percentage is. And you get a bit of a budget to reskill yourself so that when you come back full-time, you haven't lost out on skills. The company is trying to create more bespoke employment contracts.

Unilever has already begun experimenting with innovative employment models. Wels offers this example:

> A senior leader told us, "I want to stay connected to Unilever." He is super passionate about executive leadership development and particularly one-on-one coaching of our top two hundred. But he also wants to work with young kids. So he's made an arrangement: part of the time, he will be connected with Unilever doing the work that he was doing; and part of the time, he will start to focus on setting up a new business for himself that's more of a social enterprise. He can pursue other dreams, and at the same time, Unilever can tap into what he has to offer and not lose out on his expertise, his passion, his purpose.

This example perfectly illustrates how organizations are modifying worker engagement models to align organizational needs with worker preferences. As has been true for many years, in some situations employees may become contractors, while in other cases contractors may become employees. Within a workforce ecosystem structure, the individual remains an integral part of the workforce ecosystem, regardless of the specific employment relationship.

From Attracting Workers for Jobs to Skills-Focused Worker Access

Executives leading the charge on orchestrating workforce ecosystems are increasingly committed to attracting candidates based on their skills and experiences rather than on job titles. At Unilever, Wels embraced this approach, noting that "to engage people in a variety of employment models, the organization selects based on skills and experiences." Wels champions the idea of data-supported "skills passports" that workers can present to potential employers to expand opportunities, noting, "We can democratize opportunities for people in a very frictionless way." Using skills-focused recruiting, for both internal movement and the recruitment of external contributors, allows organizations to better match candidates with opportunities.

The recent shift to remote work has accelerated the skills-based engagement of contributors in all types of arrangements and without regard to location, broadening organizations' available talent pools.

These new ways of engaging exist across employment models, encompassing employees, contractors, gig workers, and even crowd contributors, creating an additional way to extend access to capabilities and insights beyond full- and part-time hiring. The University of Michigan's Dave Ulrich sees boundless possibilities with these new trends. "I see companies saying, 'I'm going where the labor legislation allows me to manage my workforce in a way that works,' especially for knowledge workers," he observes. "'I'm going to start getting my knowledge workers from Sri Lanka, from Singapore, from India. I don't have to hire people who went to Berkeley or Harvard. I can hire people from anywhere.' We're seeing the global marketplace redefine what we do."

In the future, companies working together could help shape the global labor marketplace. Unilever's U-Work initiative aims to create consortia with other companies to develop labor pools comprising people who are now working for Unilever and yet may become less in demand as the company shifts its business model. According to Wels, "Unilever might need less, say, manufacturing skills, but other environments do need the skills Unilever's people have." Initiatives like these will allow companies to help their employees while continuing to fine-tune their own workforce ecosystems.

Skills-focused hiring practices can also help organizations access skills concentrated in specific demographics. An internship program at one company we studied offers young people the opportunity to rotate apprenticeships throughout the company before being hired for specific jobs. Referring to the younger generation's "TikTok skill set," an executive says, "Our organization is tapping into talent earlier in careers to use skills that are more naturally coming from the younger generation while plugging them into a more seasoned, experienced organization. The collision of this next generation workforce with very different skills, coupled with the experience of our existing workforce is what will enable us to deliver the products of the future for our clients." This example illustrates how workforce ecosystem strategy can help drive business strategy. Accessing workers with new skills via an ecosystem approach, the organization is able to expand the comprehensiveness of its resources, build community, and provide a wider range of offerings to clients.

Moreover, this enhanced focus on skills in workforce ecosystems invites (and begins to require) new ways to ensure that an individual has a particular skill, not just a particular experience. As attracting people with specific skills and credentials becomes necessary, employers will need to be able to credibly and reliably authenticate the skills that workers claim to have. As we discussed in chapter 7, companies like Manpower and iDatafy are using new technologies such as blockchain to verify candidates easily and in seconds.

Using Opportunity Markets and Labor Platforms

In an effort to access workers with the right skills for the right tasks or projects rather than merely fill job openings, many companies are experimenting with talent markets and seeking contingent workers through external digital labor platforms.

Opportunity Markets

Organizations are increasingly aware that they can align their interests and their workers' interests, and thus improve retention, by providing workers with new opportunities. Meeting an enterprise's need for new skills is different and distinct from enabling opportunities for workers to have new experiences as well as to develop and apply valued skills. The executives we spoke with consistently asserted that they felt the best way to accomplish the former was by committing to the latter. They emphasize the importance of providing opportunities so that workers can develop in ways that both they and the company value. Opportunity marketplaces, which connect workers with short-term projects and other areas of need within the organization, offer a mechanism for achieving that. At Schneider Electric, executives observe that attrition has decreased in areas where they've launched an opportunity market.

Schneider Electric methodically seeks input from employees about which skills they're most interested in acquiring. It also maintains a continually updated system of reference that catalogs the skills necessary for each job organization-wide. The company intends to use analytics to identify what skills are in demand, what skills employees want to learn, and what skills are becoming less relevant. The workforce opportunities that Schneider offers will be informed by that data. Effective opportunity marketplaces efficiently match an employer's demand for skills with a supply of opportunities that connect with employee interests.

Using internal talent markets to better categorize and access skills and capabilities from existing employees is an increasingly common approach. But the demand for workers is so great that a growing number of organizations are planning to open many of these internal markets to external contributors as well, growing their workforce ecosystems beyond their organizational boundaries. For example, another business we studied created an internal talent marketplace that a manager describes as "talent deal-making." He explains, "As parts of our business need more project management support or expertise, we're creating a really productive skills and capability brokerage that's the catalyst for your next curation or your next gig inside the company." The company is planning to open the marketplace to external workers, which will essentially link the internal employee model with the broader workforce ecosystem model, providing much more comprehensive orchestration of the entire structure.

In a similar spirit, Swiss health care multinational Roche is piloting an integrated gig/project marketplace that matches opportunities with an employee's skills and interests. Part of the intention is to break down organizational silos and boundaries. "The important topic for us is to what extent we can swarm people to where their capabilities would enable us to solve very complicated problems as efficiently and effectively as possible," notes Cristina Wilbur. "It's no longer being concerned about reporting lines and hierarchy, but rather this notion of networks." The expanded marketplace provides access to capabilities and connections among different types of workers.

Susan Podlogar says that MetLife is using its talent marketplace to eliminate bureaucracy, deliver new experiences, and alter people's thinking about how work gets done. "Not only are we getting access to talent to meet critical needs, we're also enabling people to expand their experiences by having different opportunities in the same organization," she says.

> It's helping our leaders and employees shift their mindset in terms of how work can get done differently. For example, we had a director post a project, and a vice president [VP] bid on it. There was no issue that a VP was now going to work for a director on a project. And the VP afterward wrote what an incredible experience it was. "I got access to a business problem that I would never have been able to work on, so now I understand the business even better." The direct and indirect positive outcomes on these things are just incredible.

Digital Labor Platforms

The proliferation of digital labor platforms—such as Upwork, Toptal, Catalant, and Freelancer—is enabling and accelerating the development of workforce ecosystems. With labor platforms, organizations can easily search for, and then flexibly engage with, external individuals and teams. They provide access to workers with skills that companies need, while lowering the cost and complexity of discovering them. Digital labor platforms represent a technology-enabled class of businesses that are integral to workforce ecosystem growth and implementation.

Researchers and worldwide policy organizations have adopted multiple definitions of digital labor platforms.[1] Harvard Business School professor Joe Fuller notes that labor platforms fall into three groups: crowdsourcing platforms, where firms solicit input on specific projects from a wide array of people, sometimes offering pay or prizes, and sometimes seeking contributions simply by asking provocative questions that people enjoy tackling; freelancer platforms, where potential workers post credentials and organizations can engage them for some unit of time; and curated online demand platforms, like Toptal or Catalant, which cater to more specific services and often higher-skilled work, and can be a channel for small groups of people or firms to offer services.[2]

These labor platforms have benefits, but also limitations. Many groups in an organization can take advantage of these platforms to address skills shortfalls or bring in workers to perform short-term projects. But this haphazard approach to enlisting external talent—reactive, local, and uncoordinated—can generate inefficiencies.[3] Graf from Novartis recalls that when he was at PepsiCo, the company ran some successful experiments with Upwork in Asia Pacific, but he points out that "the question is always, How do you scale it so that you mobilize a workforce of fifty thousand? And possibly even more over time?" Solving the scale issue, especially for large organizations, often requires a coordinated, centralized approach. Engaging in strategic relationships with labor platforms to manage large groups of contingent workers is one potential solution. These engagements may be outgrowths of long-standing alliances with staffing agencies that have become more digitally enabled or new associations with more recently emergent platforms.

The Employee Life Cycle in Context

Despite all the changes, many aspects of the employee life cycle will—and should—continue for the foreseeable future in some organizations, even as they build workforce ecosystems. Some companies will continue to rely on employees as much as possible to get work done, and this is fitting in certain contexts. Highly employee-centric approaches may be appropriate, for example, when secrecy is of paramount importance or in instances where the majority of positions are so specialized that they take years to master. In those cases, companies will continue to focus on attracting, developing, and retaining employees, and employee continuity will remain critical.

Ceridian is a company that believes that employees will remain at the heart of their organization for the foreseeable future. As Julie Derene explains, "My bias is to make the most use out of the part- and full-time workforce before turning to the external workforce, in part due to the importance of that internal workforce to retention and engagement." Her colleague, CHRO Tohyama, agrees: "The key is always going to be, a company has a product, and you have to have a core team of people who understand that product. Can you supplement that with people who have external expertise and different points of view? Absolutely.

But in my view, you have to always have a core group of people who truly understand what your product is, what your culture is, and make sure that you're not betraying or straying from that." Ceridian is not alone in believing in the importance of a core group of workers with an ongoing connection to the company's product. Yet our research suggests that more and more companies are coming to believe that the employee life cycle model is not the most effective organizing principle for managing complex, interdependent, and diverse workforce ecosystems.

Further Considerations

Companies have many systems, processes, and mechanisms for discovering, accessing, and engaging different types of workers and other contributors for value creation activities. It is not simply that companies are changing whom they would like to attract—that is, the types of contributors they need to access. They are also managing a much wider variety of employment engagements. Long-term employment remains a real focus, but it's no longer true that work contributors must be people with contracts of any kind. A participant could be an organization, volunteer, or technology. As the sources of value creation proliferate, leaders require a much more expansive approach than the antiquated employee life cycle model of attracting workers and contributors.

What's more, companies aren't just trying to attract great workers; they are taking intentional steps to becoming attractive themselves to a wider range of workers (see table 8.1). We heard time and again from executives that they are trying to increase their companies' appeal to the most desirable skilled workers and third-party organizations. They also hope to interest complementors in building products and services that work with theirs; for example, companies that have marketplaces or app stores are aiming to have sellers and developers join them, and invest in products (e.g., apps) that work with theirs. In sum, orchestrating workforce ecosystems requires organizations first and foremost to be able to access and attract all types of people and partners as they strive to reach their strategic goals.

Table 8.1

Management practices shifts: Accessing workforce ecosystem members

	Traditional employee life cycle approach	Workforce ecosystem approach
Workforce planning	• Limited to full- and part-time positions • Based on predictable hiring for jobs with stable skills and requirements • Traditional recruitment sources	• Uses broad definition of extended workforce, including human and digital workforces • All workforce contributor types for all work requirements across all sources
Workforce acquisition	• HR manages talent acquisition, with employee role-based hiring • Procurement and IT manage service providers to augment workforce • Legal manages contracts for many employment models • Each department manages talent requirements beyond full-time equivalents (FTEs) in silos	• HR works with other functions to coordinate acquisition and access; focus is on work types, not roles • Shift to skills-focused hiring • Ample leveraging of opportunity markets and digital labor platforms for access • Workforce analytics offer a consolidated view of internal *and* external workforces (e.g., people, partners, and technologies)

Action Questions

1. Does your organization's workforce planning process include partnering and other methods to gain access to people and partners in addition to traditional employee acquisition processes?

2. As you consider workforce planning, does your organization include various types of external contributors and diverse employment models (including engaging with third-party subcontractors, service providers, independent consultants, and long- and short-term contractors)?

3. From where is your organization accessing these resources? Are these the most appropriate sources? Is your organization fully leveraging new modes of worker and partner acquisition such as digital labor platforms?

9 Aligning Interests with Workforce Ecosystems

In most large groups, keeping participants feeling respected and engaged leads to much better outcomes than the alternative. In the context of workforce ecosystems, this translates into making sure all participants can achieve their own individual goals as well as contributing to collective ones. The traditional employee life cycle model includes "develop" as the second tenet, implying an emphasis on training employees for a career path for the organization's benefit. But orchestrating a workforce ecosystem requires an expanded version of this notion—one that allows contributors to develop in ways that may be beneficial beyond their role for a particular organization. Additionally, while the employee life cycle model includes "retention" as its final tenet, a new interpretation focuses instead on aligning interests. Though there may be times when worker retention remains a high priority for an organization, there also could be occasions when an organization's shifting priorities call for increased fluidity and flexibility, possibly in direct opposition to a retention approach. An organization may find it more appropriate to have a structure that at least in part, can change according to its needs, varying who and what contributes to developing and delivering its products and services.

In this chapter we continue our discussion of management practices associated with orchestrating a workforce ecosystem. These shifts not only support an organization in reaching its strategic goals but also in developing growth opportunities for workforce ecosystem participants.

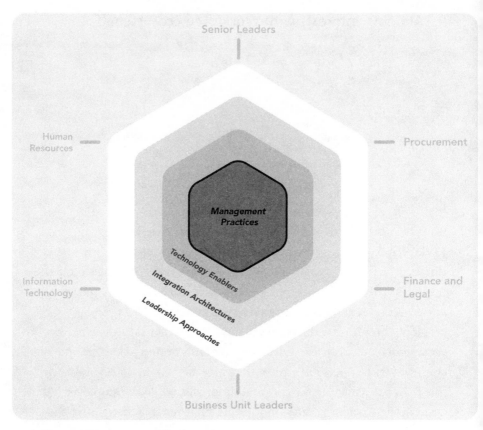

Figure 9.1
Management practices in the workforce ecosystem orchestration framework.

As in chapter 8, these practices are reflected by the centermost hexagon in our workforce ecosystem orchestration framework (see figure 9.1). In the following sections, we consider learning and development, career planning, performance management, and organizational alignment as they relate to orchestrating workforce ecosystems.

Learning and Development

In many organizations, learning and development activities have shifted from being driven by a top-down model structured to benefit the company, to one that offers more options and opportunities for growth to a wider array of workers. In the employee life cycle approach, training is provided for specific job requirements, organization compliance, and security needs. Manager nomination and enterprise requirements regulate learning, which is often siloed by function and division, and limited to employees.

In a workforce ecosystem, on the other hand, learning and development is more accessible, and serves a broader purpose. It becomes a more continuous, more self-directed, and inclusive activity that applies to a wider variety of workers, such as employees, other contributors, and even potential contributors. Development in workforce ecosystems is less about developing workers for the company and more about helping workers grow so they are more valuable, both to themselves *and* the company.

Companies like Walmart, Ceridian, and Unilever seek to unlock the potential of all members of the workforce ecosystem, not only to create value for the organization, but to create value for workers also. For these companies, workers' development is not just about benefiting the organization by improving its inventory of skills, nor need it be about enhancing a worker's day-to-day job performance or overall career trajectory at the company. Development needn't even revolve around a worker's skills; it could include creating novel experiences such as a rotation assignment to work within a client or supplier organization for a short time, or the opportunity to easily move to another division on a temporary basis. In a workforce ecosystem, developing workers solely "for the company" shifts to helping workers advance to achieve a potential of their choosing. In this environment, "We each become the agent of our own opportunity," asserts Walmart's Donna Morris.

Julie Derene says that Ceridian has introduced what the company calls "pervasive learning," in which learning is embedded into work. The company offers everything from traditional development and job shadowing to microskill building and short-burst technology training—"things that give workers what they need in real time." Ceridian's approach affords workers the opportunity to acquire the training they need when they need it, supporting their ability to direct their own development.

Unilever proactively offers training opportunities to help workers develop specific skills for more in-demand roles. "The company is trying to make matches to show people their current skill set," Jeroen Wels says. "With a little bit of additional training, a little bit of additional investment in yourself, how can you build a better proposition for yourself to go for the jobs that are in high demand in the very near future?" Unilever doesn't require employees to take the training; rather, it identifies training that can support workers to develop their potential.

At Schneider Electric, employees are the ones taking a proactive approach to identifying desirable new skills to learn. "We don't necessarily identify the skills that employees need to learn," notes Andrew Saidy, the company's former vice president of talent digitization. "Employees do that for us." At Schneider, employees can seek out new projects, gigs, and roles on the company's internal talent marketplace. These types of marketplaces don't merely match business requirements with workers' skill and experience. They also connect those requirements with workers' ambitions and interests as well as their potential to learn and grow.

Providing Growth Opportunities for Workforce Ecosystem Participants
As a workforce ecosystem expands, some companies offer ecosystem participants wide access to relevant training, affording them opportunities to upskill or reskill, and grow their capabilities and scope of expertise. This in turn allows companies to attract and build a large skilled community of potential contributors. In some cases, as with Applause's uTest network of testers, anyone can register to become a member of the community and enroll in free training, whether or not the company has assigned the individual to an actual revenue-generating project. (We've experienced this firsthand; after discussing Applause's approach to community building and training with the CEO, one of the authors registered to be a member of the tester network and was

able to participate in the community-wide training.) Randstad Sourcer-ight's Mike Smith describes a similar perspective at one of the com-pany's clients: "It wants to give rejected candidates the ability to have access to microskills or learning that are available through the com-pany's internal LMS [learning management system]. So the next time a job comes around, they have an increased propensity to apply for it and be able to get that assignment."

Embarking on a different approach, but still focused on expanding training opportunities across a workforce ecosystem, one business we studied has codeveloped certifications with partners including Adobe, Salesforce, Amazon, and Facebook for their own employees as well as freelancers. The training and certifications are provided by the partners, and benefit both the company itself and the freelancers. The business can promote the certifications as part of its value proposition to clients; freelancers gain access to free training that increases their desirability both within this organization's workforce ecosystem and with potential other employers. In the program's first six months, more than twenty thousand people were certified.

This same company is also reaching out to a potential workforce of future employees with a virtual learning program, which helps young people develop necessary skills and experiences. The program was con-ceived after the COVID-19 pandemic forced the business to cancel its in-person internships in 2020. Switching to remote, the company was able to expand the program globally; they ended up with nine hundred participants from twenty-seven countries—a much larger cohort with a broader global reach than it had originally planned for the in-person program. As one of their executives said, "There are nine hundred more advocates for our company and our industry in the world right now, and that really didn't cost a lot of money."

In the same vein, Novartis is extending opportunities to its external contributors. "Over time we've moved from, let's leave external workers at arm's length to managing them more closely and bringing the cul-ture closer to them," explains Markus Graf. "We're also enrolling them in our learning and development offerings. A concrete example is that we granted access to LinkedIn Learning so they can benefit from access to learning opportunities. We're going to see more of that as more is enabled through technology."

As these novel practices emerge, they raise questions pertaining to risk and responsibility. An executive we interviewed captures some of the issues yet to be resolved. She asks,

> With contingent workers typically employed through a third party but residing in the ecosystem of the company, what's our responsibility to provide them with opportunities to grow skills? And what's the third-party employer's responsibility in that space?" The bias at our company is to be more inclusive than not. But it's about how you define the employment relationship and where you balance risk around the contingent workforce with the fact that really, at the end of the day, they're an extended part of your workforce. If your desire is to be as inclusive as possible to develop that external workforce, where's the boundary where the risk becomes too great?

In a workforce ecosystem, companies have many choices around their approach to contributors' growth. Businesses can, but need not, make learning management systems available to all comers, for instance. Most executives we spoke with found that a more inclusive approach to development has several benefits, including attracting desirable workers (for now and possibly for the future) with needed skills. As ServiceNow's Canney observes, "The idea of openness and building capability in the outer rings and the inner rings of the workforce is an internal strategy and an ecosystem strategy." Still, it's certainly possible to take a less inclusive approach to worker development that caters less to the preferences and interests of all ecosystem participants. This may seem like a more economical move in the short term, but over time, in a world where organizations pay a premium for available skilled workers, building a community of ready, willing, and able workers may prove to be the more profitable route. Leaders orchestrating workforce ecosystems should weigh the trade-offs for each approach, considering which is most suitable for their context over both the short- and long-term.

Career Planning

We've heard loud and clear that our people not only want a variety of work experiences but they also want to be invested with the kind of growth opportunity in both skills and experiences along whatever path they create for themselves.

—Jacqui Canney, ServiceNow

When leaders manage with an eye toward unleashing workers' potential, career paths open up. A salesperson moves into product development; a finance manager moves to HR to influence DE&I efforts; a marketing analyst moves to sourcing to concentrate on sustainability and climate. Ceridian's Susan Tohyama reports that the company's global polling found that more than half of employees would opt for a lateral move, or even a lesser role, to gain new skills and experiences.

Workforce ecosystems enable those choices by making opportunities for workers available and, importantly, visible; at the same time, they create new benefits for the organization. Tohyama, reflecting on Ceridian's internal talent marketplace, observes that nowadays, "employees are not necessarily chasing titles. They're chasing experiences. They're looking for building experience value within their career, not just title value."

This shift has meaningful implications for how workers and businesses are defining as well as managing careers. The metaphor of the career ladder is being replaced by more multidirectional, wide-ranging terms, such as portfolios, lattices, jungle gyms, climbing walls, and lane changes. University of Michigan's Dave Ulrich says he uses the term *mosaic* in his consulting practice. "The mosaic means I can move all over," he notes. "We had four stages: individual, contributor, manager, and director. Now you have a mosaic that allows you to move horizontally, vertically, down, sideways, inside, and out. The mosaic allows you to create a very different career."

Ulrich further suggests conceiving of careers less in terms of nouns (roles and titles) than of verbs (exploring new experiences, building

new skills, and discovering new opportunities). "The role doesn't matter as much as the action," he says. "We often define ourselves by role,
but that isn't what you do. What do you do? You accelerate business.
You advance human capability. You mobilize information. You explore
ideas. We've been tilted to the noun. I think we want to tilt a little bit
to the verb."

Rethinking Career Management
In a workforce ecosystem, the entire notion of career management
demands rethinking. "With career management, I think the word
management probably is wrong already," Jeroen Wels asserts. "We start
from a place where we had careers managed by function, which are,
by definition, silos. But you go from strong silo functions to a world
where large parts of the functions will be broken through or nonexis-
tent. They are going to be replaced with what we can call 'beehives of
skills,' the skill sets that you need to get work done, depending on what
the value is that you want to create." The shift from workers following
a proscribed path to determining their own growth and direction is a
material change, both for workers and companies.

"What I'm trying to change is that you curate yourself," explains
a leader at one company we studied. "You can be an employee of our
company and know that you could pick a client, pick a brand, pick
a technology, whatever inspires you, and not have to leave the family. But right now, it's not very easy to move around without barriers.
That's the stuff we're trying to take down." For companies like this one,
careers aren't to be managed by the organization as much as they're to
be curated or navigated by workers themselves.

There is a cost to ignoring workers' interests around directing their
own career trajectories. In the past, Deutsche Post DHL Group required
employees to remain in their jobs for a year before they were eligible
to apply for new jobs internally. These regulations weren't serving the
organization well, as DPDHL Group found itself losing people. "We
decided to do a fundamental shift and say no more functional streams,
no more linear processes," recalls Meredith Wellard, vice president of

group learning, talent, and HR platforms. "Let's go to skills. Let's talk about what skills you have, and then we'll make it visible that you might be someone who could take this internal job. And we make it visible the other way around, where we say to the leader, here's the next three people who might be suitable for a job that you've got open in your team."

Openness and flexibility are now central to employees' career planning at DPDHL Group. As Wellard puts it,

> At the core of our career marketplaces is a belief that we need to shift from functional silo-based talent planning and management toward a much more skills-based and flexible marketplace that's a lot more open and employee driven. We remove the barriers to mobility that have existed from legacy approaches. In our marketplace, skills are the currency that you're trading, and access to your data is the fundamental price of entry. When you decide, yes, make my data visible and then put the skills into the mix, then you will have access to opportunities, learning, growth, succession, and a genuine opportunity to have a cradle-to-grave career with Deutsche Post DHL Group.

Essentially, DPDHL Group is aiming to build an information system that includes all of a worker's relevant information—work experiences, ratings and rankings, skill certifications, and so on—to allow the marketplace to provide the most appropriate opportunity matches.

Enabling Flexible Careers

These days, workers are less likely to aspire to remain at a single company for their entire professional career. Tomas Chamorro-Premuzic of ManpowerGroup points out that many workers today have messy and heterogeneous profiles with a mix of full-time, consulting, and extracurricular gigs. He warns that "if you want to retain and engage people and keep them motivated, you have to be willing to make compromises and be more flexible. More people are managing their careers as a portfolio than before."

We mentioned in chapter 8 that Unilever is experimenting with creating consortia of companies to facilitate employees having opportunities at multiple organizations. Similarly, Seagate was in the early stages of exploring a system of cross-company employee sharing. "One of the things that was being discussed was how we tag onto a network or a consortium of companies that also have marketplaces where we can have a fluid ecosystem of talent sharing across organizations—when it makes sense for our business," says Andrew Saidy, former global head of talent and learning at the data storage company. "The idea is not very mature yet. We are interested in exploring how we can connect with the external talent world."

As we noted earlier, one company we know is considering a talent-sharing program that it believes will be beneficial for all parties involved. For instance, a client with openings in one division might ask the company to loan it some people for a period to save the client the time and investment necessary to fill the positions. The client would be able to fill the role with a partner they trust, the company would be able to solidify and deepen the relationship with the client, and the employee would gain new experiences.

In a workforce ecosystem, the meaning and management of careers—for both organizations and workers—become more varied and variable. We see companies experimenting with a wide range of flexible alternatives as they orchestrate workforce ecosystems. These alternatives actively address the preferences of all members of the workforce ecosystem and support workers of all types as they take ownership over their career trajectories. Many leaders believe that developing the potential of workers—whether they stay with their companies or not—will have long-term benefits for their workforce ecosystems.

From Performance Management to Coaching Performance

As they move to orchestrating workforce ecosystems, a growing number of companies are rejecting or heavily modifying the much-maligned annual performance review, with its focus on assessing individual employees' past performance toward specific goals.[1] At its best in these contexts, performance management is becoming more prospective (rather than retrospective), more developmental (versus evaluative), more team oriented (as opposed to exclusively individual oriented), more continuous (rather than periodic), and more self-directed (instead of management driven).

The old systems of performance management don't serve organizations (or ecosystem participants) well when managers are orchestrating multiple internal and external workforces, including people, organizations, and technologies. Nevertheless, to unlock the potential of all workers, internal and external, managers must have systems and processes in place to continuously improve performance. As Ulrich says, "You've got to build work systems for people whether they're full-time, part-time, or outside. You still need to think about performance management. You've got to build accountability for delivery; you've got to build incentives."

These incentives need not always be financial. For example, in workforce ecosystems where crowdsourcing or innovation contests are in use, participants engage in ranking and reputational systems where they can exchange feedback and build marketable portfolios. Credentials of all sorts, including badges, digital certificates, NFTs, and others, serve as valuable compensation for some contributors. The scope of performance management expands, applying to employees, teams, other contributors (both individuals and teams), and even employers (consider online systems that rank workplaces, for instance).

Finally, complicating performance management even further, not all workers will be under a manager's direct supervision, especially in cases where third-party subcontractors are involved. Morris describes a scenario in which Walmart fulfills an order for a customer and prepares it for delivery. "If I'm using a third party to deliver it and that's a disaster, you're not going to care that it's a third party—you're going to just care that it's Walmart," she reasons. Customers aren't interested in hearing about the structure of an organization, and who may be directly employed or not; from their perspective, whoever (and/or whatever) touches the product or service represents the company whose brand is on it. Walmart, and every other organization orchestrating a workforce ecosystem, needs to measure the performance of individual and organizational contributors while being sure those metrics align with strategic goals and objectives.

From Retention to Aligning Interests

As we noted at the start of this chapter, the third pillar in the generally accepted, traditional "attract, develop, and retain" model of employee life cycle management assumes that organizations wish to retain the vast majority of the individuals working for them (which is not always the case for myriad reasons); it also focuses narrowly on financial compensation and benefits to retain valuable workers.

Companies orchestrating workforce ecosystems often take a more expansive approach to engaging with their contributors and consider many types of engagement models. They aim to align corporate interests with those of individual workers and other value creators. No consensus yet exists on how best to accommodate all members of the workforce ecosystem in this emerging vision of more comprehensive opportunities, rewards, and benefits.

Understanding how workers think about trade-offs between financial remuneration and freedom can help companies align compensation practices with the interests of workers both inside and outside the company. Jill Popelka, author of *Experience, Inc.* and former SAP SuccessFactors president, observes, "The contingent workers I speak to are very independent, and they want freedom. They believe freedom is a fair exchange for not having full benefits. But we have to continue to deliberately listen to them as we move forward. If they value benefits, then maybe we need to think more creatively about how we structure benefits." PlanOmatic is already moving in this direction. CEO Kori Covrigaru acknowledges that the company loses contractors (known as PlanOtechs) over benefits. "I would say the number one reason we lose PlanOtechs is because they find a full-time job with health benefits," he says. "You can't compete with that. People need benefits. They need health care. Part of our vision is to be able to offer basic benefits to our contractor network."

Purposeful Alignment

Recognizing that individuals are searching for more meaning in their lives, many companies adopting a workforce ecosystem approach are aligning their commitments to growth and value creation with workers' interests in meaningful work and other interests extending beyond financial renumeration. Relatedly, within workforce ecosystems, retaining workers in long-term employment arrangements may not be a primary goal either for workers or companies. The emphasis moves to meaningful engagement during a specific time frame. "We have to understand, it's not always loyalty that we can retain someone for years; the need may just be for a shorter engagement," says MetLife's Susan Podlogar. "So, for that period of time, no matter the duration, how do I have the worker fully committed and aligned to the objectives and outcomes? For us, all we do starts with purpose. We attract people who are motivated by who we are and what we contribute to the world. Our purpose is 'always with you, building a more confident future.' That is energizing, when you know you can contribute to confident futures for millions of people around the world in some of their most trying times." Instead of concentrating exclusively on retention, MetLife seeks to align an individual's pursuit of meaningful work with the company's pursuit of its corporate purpose.

NIKE, Inc., SolarWinds, and WorkBoard board member Cathy Benko notes that it's essential to create a culture that aligns corporate and personal values with meaningful contributions. "The common denominator is culture," she asserts.

> People are making different choices about where they live and work, and how they engage in a workplace. Turnover is significantly higher across the board, but the inflow of people is also high. They're calling it "the great swap." Within that swap, you have to figure out the cohesion and the ties that bind—the things that held us together for all of those years besides

economic interests. If you don't figure that out, employees will become mercenary if they're working from home and doing Zoom or coding or whatever, without all of those intangibles that produce some of a psychic reward to work. You're part of a team, you're making something happen, you're making good on a purpose. You have to figure out how to do that in this ecosystem.

Wels, formerly of Unilever, describes the current shift in management models this way: "We are moving away from, 'You shall do this . . .' to 'You need to follow your purpose and build experiences that you will be good at.' What type of skills do they want to build? What fits with their purpose? It's a shift to constantly looking to guide people toward the career that they aspire to."

At NASA, Nicholas Skytland says the agency endeavors to make sure all members of the workforce ecosystem feel tied to the organization rather than feeling like cogs in a machine. "The problem with the gig economy is that in the name of capitalism or business or efficiency, we forget there are humans at the core of this whole thing," he reflects. "Humans have needs. We want to belong. We want to identify with organizations. We want to relate to others. We want safety and security, and we want to be incentivized in a way that's motivating to us." Skytland notes that the connection between workers and the agency's mission is its top priority. "It drives the entire future-of-work framework," he says. Meaningful work can be linked directly to purpose and opportunities for growth that workers may want to pursue within a company's ecosystem.

Closing Thoughts

The transition from development in the employee life cycle to the growth and advancement of human potential in workforce ecosystems calls for a new set of management practices. This doesn't mean that the type of development in the employee life cycle has no place in workforce ecosystems: career ladders will continue to exist, and people will climb them. Rather, workforce ecosystems expand the range of growth options and investments, on the part of both workers and the organization. The key difference is that workforce ecosystems enable many kinds of workers to have greater choice and stronger agency over how they advance their potential. Workforce ecosystems recognize and reflect the budding reality of portfolio careers with lifelong reinvention.

Similarly, it is clear that retention will continue to play a significant role in how management engages employees. The costs of replacing an employee remain high—anywhere from 50 percent to twice an employee's annual salary.[2] Employee expertise and tacit knowledge regarding a company's products, services, and systems can be a source of competitive advantage. Retention still matters. In a workforce ecosystem, however, the nature and scope of retention efforts may change. Compensation broadens to include skills development, new opportunities, and more options for meaningful work. Financial compensation still matters, of course, but as workers seek more from their work experience, many are willing to exchange financial opportunities for other types. Compensation increasingly becomes future oriented—a shift from rewarding past performance. In sum, we see companies diversifying their compensation tactics as they reconsider retention methods anchored to the employee life cycle.

More broadly, this discussion highlights a point sometimes taken for granted: the purpose of retention is usually (and largely) to align a company's interests with those of a specific group of workers (i.e., employees). But when corporate interests become aligned with a broader array of workers with a more diverse set of interests, the nature of retention as well as compensation shifts. What's more, when corporate interests are less about increasing production from employees and more about achieving more valuable outcomes from a workforce ecosystem, the nature of compensation and the purpose of retention shift further.

Table 9.1 below consolidates the many shifts in management practices that occur when transitioning from the outdated employee life cycle to a workforce ecosystem model. This view shows the wide range of changes we have discussed in chapters 8–9.

Table 9.1

Management practices shifts: Developing growth opportunities and aligning interests

	Traditional employee life cycle approach	Workforce ecosystem approach
Learning and development	• Provided for specific job, compliance, and security requirements • Regulated by manager nomination and enterprise requirements • Siloed by function and division • Limited to internal audiences	• Development and growth are key focus areas • Aligning skills, capabilities, and competencies with future organizational needs, changing business strategies, and skill requirements • High degree of worker-driven options • Offerings consider requirements and expectations of internal *and* external workers • Workforce analytics platforms provide consolidated view of internal *and* external workforce learning requirements and progress
Career planning	• Organizations follow linear, hierarchical career paths based on functions and business units • Mentorship programs are offered ad hoc and as needed • Structured rotation programs move small cohorts (and small percentages of employees) to build experiences within the organization	• Internal and external talent marketplaces reveal worker interests and experiences as well as unlock opportunities • Worker preferences drive agency and choice for multidirectional career opportunities • Fractionalized and project-based work offers opportunities • Opportunities available outside the organization for growth experiences
Performance management	• Annual goals set by standard roles focusing on full-time equivalents • Individual performance metrics based on standard role requirements • Retrospective view and limited team focus	• Continuous goal setting and feedback • Focus on improving performance and development for internal *and* external contributors • Integrated approach to evaluating internal *and* external workforce for contributions, growth, and development

Table 9.1 (continued)

	Traditional employee life cycle approach	Workforce ecosystem approach
Retention and aligning interests	• Focused on full- and part-time employees, and concerned with pay, benefits, and user experience of HR systems • Loosely connected to emerging initiatives such as DE&I programs • Focus on retention	• Expanded and holistic view of employee and workforce experience • Extends beyond salary and benefits to personal growth along with access to jobs and projects • Alignment of personal and work-life balance including location (remote work), job choice, and personal with corporate purpose

Action Questions

1. To what extent are learning and development activities in your organization's workforce ecosystem tied to a standard career progression that may no longer be relevant to many of the people who create value for your organization?

2. Can employees and external workers access development and growth activities (and experiences) to prepare for and perform productively in the work your organization needs to accomplish to reach its strategic goals? How does one need to be engaged with the organization to take advantage of learning opportunities?

3. Can your organization's extended workforce easily see opportunities to move ahead in their current roles? Can they move to new divisions and/or functions, and accelerate their advancement to leadership roles?

4. Do compensation, benefits, and reward structures adequately address the diversity of employment relationships across the workforce ecosystem, including people, partners, and technologies? Do they reflect the values of your organization and communities?

5. How can you rethink your organization's management practices to focus on improving and fueling performance and growth, not just managing tasks, behaviors, workflows, and processes? Can your organization use any external sources for performance management such as ranking or reputation systems?

III Developing Socially Responsible Workforce Ecosystems

10 Ethics in Workforce Ecosystems

Moving from an employee-based workforce to a workforce ecosystem has ethical implications. The ethical treatment of *employees*, for example, is often well articulated and well communicated, with well-established systems of accountability, especially in large, public companies. The norms, values, and expectations around what a company owes its employees are typically knowable, even if the company doesn't always live up to them. But once a broader set of contributors is considered, ethical obligations become harder to articulate and communicate, and accountability becomes less systematized.[1]

To understand and address this shift, leaders need to consider these three questions at the very least:

1. What are our ethical responsibilities toward a workforce that extends beyond—sometimes far beyond—our organizational boundaries?

2. How do we make our workforce ecosystems fair and inclusive for both internal employees and external contributors?

3. How will we support and promote ethical behavior across our workforce ecosystem?

Worker safety is a practical use case for exploring the first question. Most organizations recognize both a legal and ethical obligation to provide a safe working environment for their employees. A company that has just begun to manage mission-critical work through a workforce ecosystem, however—either by choice or necessity—may not apply the same safety principles for contingent workers as for its own employees.

While its practices may comply with the law, having different standards of safety for employees and other contributors can bring criticism that tarnishes the company's brand and/or hinders its ability to attract top talent.

DE&I practices offer a useful perspective on the second question. They represent several important ethical principles. DE&I practices can improve access to opportunities among historically underrepresented groups.[2] What's more, they typically embrace principles that consider all people, regardless of gender, race, age, wealth, and cognitive capability, as deserving respect. DE&I then connects with two key elements of ethics: the right and the good.

Few companies have diversity objectives for both employees and contingent laborers.[3] Staffing agencies can help provide some information and support goal setting, but it remains challenging to assess DE&I in a global market environment. Among multinationals, for example, it is difficult to determine what the appropriate benchmark should be to inform diversity goal setting in local markets. In today's business environment, though, workers can be anywhere; companies may need to reconsider diversity benchmarks in a workforce ecosystem.

Many companies are beginning to grapple with how far they should go toward "including" contingent workers. Some are leaning toward a more inclusive approach in which every worker—whatever they do or however long they do it for—is a prospective brand ambassador. But this approach doesn't explain *what* a contingent worker is being "included" in. Is it the company's culture generally? Its community? Its brand? The specific team that the worker participates in? Answers to these questions are obvious for an employee: it's the company and all that goes along with that. Yet the answers are less obvious for contingent workers. How will companies define and implement "inclusion" across the workforce ecosystem? How will inclusion practices avoid unequal treatment? As Chandra Sanders, director of RISE, a scholarship program at the digital talent marketplace the Mom Project, told us, "A lot of time contingent workers are perceived as second-class citizens in the workplace. A culture shift has to happen to ensure that contingent workers are heard. Many times, contingent workers can't even speak up."

Few companies are currently addressing the third question, regarding how to support and promote ethical behavior in a workforce ecosystem. Most companies have a functional role—a chief counsel's office—for managing legal responsibilities and ensuring compliance with existing laws. This office typically includes a dedicated team of workers who keep up with changes to the law and track business activities to ensure compliance with, say, local labor laws governing relationships between companies and contingent workers. But companies do not have a comparable functional role dedicated to managing ethical responsibilities for a workforce ecosystem.

A growing number of companies have a chief ethics officer role, but this role is more the exception than the rule, and seems to be generally focused on the behaviors and activities of the organization and its employees. Do companies need a single person or group to be responsible for ethical behavior across their workforce ecosystem? If not, how should a business preempt, identify, and rectify exploitation of its extended workforce? In community-oriented workforce ecosystems, for example, a duty of care naturally arises when contingent workers are considered "part of the family," "part of the community," or "included in the culture." The more inclusive and community oriented a workforce ecosystem is, the more demanding its ethical responsibilities become. An employee-centric code of conduct is unlikely to suffice.

Ethical responsibilities within a workforce ecosystem extend far beyond those for individual workers. They also include ethical conduct among interdependent organizations. For instance, the pharmaceutical company Regeneron settled with the federal government after it (along with other pharma companies) was discovered to be paying health care foundations to subsidize copays for its (and only its) drugs in direct violation of the law.[4] By deceiving customers and the government, Regeneron also failed to meet its ethical obligations to the market.

Ethical considerations are a two-way street: employers have ethical responsibilities to workers, and contingent workers have ethical responsibilities to their employers. One example concerns cybersecurity. Many contingent workers have access to sensitive data. The expectations and requirements for what they themselves can do with the data will usually be spelled out clearly. But they may also bear responsibility for protecting the data from cybercriminals, and this responsibility may be less clearly spelled out. Creating accountability for contingent workers around cybersecurity is often necessary, especially in the defense industry.

Ethical Responsibilities to Workers across the Workforce Ecosystem

In a workforce ecosystem, ethical responsibilities to workers can be influenced by whether contingent workers are hired through agencies or directly by a company. Consider Facebook's efforts to moderate problematic content, such as misinformation, obscenities, and violence. Managing problematic content is not a new problem for Facebook, but it has created a new set of ethical challenges.

Content Moderation at Facebook (Now Meta)
The *Social Network* movie popularized Facebook's origin story: Mark Zuckerberg, then a sophomore at Harvard, used software to scrape images of female students from the university's student directories and created a process that allowed students to rank the women on their looks on the website facemash.com. It became so popular, so quickly, it crashed Zuckerberg's computer. That was in 2003.

By 2007, millions of people a month were joining Facebook. Many were uploading naked pictures. The flood of pornography got the attention of the attorney general from New York. A settlement between the state and Facebook required the company to take down improper photos within a day. That mandate overwhelmed Facebook's own employees, who couldn't keep up with the deluge of images. Keeping Facebook's broad community safe became too much for Facebook's smaller community of employees.

The company subsequently created AI solutions to identify offensive material. But the AI—even as it became more sophisticated—was never 100 percent effective. Facebook's technology and employees together were not enough. In response, the company started hiring hundreds and then thousands of contract workers to moderate the content. By 2018, fifteen thousand content moderators were working on this problem for Facebook. Most moderators were hired through consulting companies and other service providers. They were trained to assess sometimes stomach-turning content such as pornography, violent images, hate speech, and other abusive material, according to a frequently changing mix of rules and policies. These workers—whose efforts were critical to the Facebook brand and its community—risked being fired if they could not achieve a 5 percent or less error rate.

The steep price for keeping the Facebook community safe went far beyond the numbers.

Agencies and other companies offered varying levels of support for the contract content moderators. Some paid the moderators paltry amounts. Others established poor working conditions. Some used a mix of their own employees and subcontractors, who were subject to unequal treatment. In other situations, there simply weren't enough moderators. Continuous exposure to the offensive content began to have psychological effects on the moderators, some of whom sought mental health support. Given the scale and scope of its contractors' work, Facebook was in a difficult position to assess and support the treatment of thousands of external workers.

A 2020 NYU study titled *Who Moderates the Social Media Giants?* revealed three main problems with Facebook's extended workforce strategy.[5] First, as the company expanded into distant countries, it did not put in place enough moderators to prevent the misuse of the platform that ultimately led to religious and ethnic violence. Second, the moderators themselves too often received inadequate support after their repeated exposure to disturbing content. Finally, the working environment for outsourced moderators was frequently chaotic, leading to disputes with quality control reviewers and other inefficiencies.

The study's key recommendation: end the contracting and hire more employees to moderate the content. Still, by February 2022, Facebook (now Meta) was continuing to contract with third parties to provide content moderation. A 2022 *TIME* magazine article detailed improper workplace practices at SAMA, a third-party content moderation facility in Nairobi, Kenya.[6] These practices included deceptive recruitment tactics, poor mental health support, and low pay, despite the fact that Facebook representatives were reported to have visited the facility to ensure compliance with the company's own standards.

Workforce ecosystems, by their very nature, encompass an extended workforce that often includes workers who have been engaged via third parties that are subcontractors to another organization. To what extent that central organization, the workforce ecosystem orchestrator, has ethical responsibilities to all the workers throughout the structure remains a difficult yet pressing question exemplified by this Facebook case.

Aligning Ethical Behaviors

The challenge of aligning ethical behaviors in a workforce ecosystem is neither new nor insuperable. It can be met through outreach, effort, investment, and commitment. Royal Dutch Shell, for instance, created a Contractor Safety Leadership initiative in 2014; the initiative acknowledges that third-party contractors perform most of the oil and gas company's high-risk work, such as offshore oil rig drilling and refinery maintenance. Shell explicitly recognizes the need to apply its company-wide safety goals—to achieve neither harm nor leaks—to its eighty thousand employees along with its entire network of contractors and third-party contributors. The company explicitly asks the question, "When working with external contractors, how can we also ensure similar high standards?"[7]

In one instance, Shell's approach to this challenge was to pair executives from twenty-one contractors with company leaders to drive safety improvements for frontline workers. Aligning the organization at many levels was key to its efforts, helping to standardize procedures to avoid complexity, confusion, and inefficiency. For one North Sea project,

Shell executives partnered with the CEO of Amec Foster Wheeler (now Wood), one of Shell's contractors, to host a series of joint workshops with staff to review safety processes. They surfaced many duplications between Shell and the contractor, which had become a source of inefficiency and confusion. The independent UK organization Step Change in Safety, which promotes safety in the oil and gas sector, is now using the partnership's approach in other North Sea projects. Shell's vice president for deep water, Ian Silk, says, "This partnership matters. If we can align on safety from the start, then the trust this builds creates a collaborative environment where people feel free to speak their minds on safety concerns."[8] Shell sees its obligations to worker safety—all workers' safety—as directly connected with its overall purpose and long-term viability.

Weyerhaeuser also relies on many contractors to complete work, and the pulp and paper company takes a similar approach to Shell's, collaborating with contractor companies and sharing requirements for effective contractor safety programs. Its approach includes risk-based safety plans that recognize and mitigate serious hazards as well as visits where Weyerhaeuser leaders join contractors on job sites to observe crews in action. The company has held a series of in-person discussions about shared values, strengths, and opportunities for improvement.[9]

Ethics and Platform Companies

Ethical obligations toward workers in a workforce ecosystem can become thornier when agencies and contractor organizations are not part of the workforce equation. Consider someone who uses a company's app to create value for themselves and the business. For example, rideshare companies such as Uber and Lyft continue to wrestle with their obligations to app users who might describe themselves as Uber or Lyft drivers (or both), but who are not legally (as of this writing) employees of either platform company.

What are a rideshare company's ethical obligations to these workers within its workforce ecosystem? The answer can be a matter of life or death. At Uber, top executives assert that safety is a top priority. In

December 2019, Uber released its first safety report, identifying 5,981 sexual assault incidents in the two-year period between 2017 and 2018. Most victims were passengers who were sexually assaulted by drivers. But drivers using the Uber platform reported being the victim in 42 percent of these assaults, which included unwanted kissing, groping, and worse.[10] There were 464 reports of rape. (Other safety issues concerned driving-related fatalities and injuries.)

The report puts these numbers into context. The Uber platform enables more than a billion rides a year globally, more than forty-five trips a second in the United States alone. Although, the actual percentage of sexual assaults per ride globally is quite low: about three incidents per million rides, these (hundreds of) rapes might not have happened without opportunities created by the Uber platform. What then is Uber's responsibility to safeguard its users?

In an interview with the *Washington Post*, CEO Dara Khosrowshahi described Uber's efforts to ensure a safe working environment for its drivers:

> We support our drivers just as we support our riders. We make sure that they have access to, first of all, all the same tools—the 911 tools, the check tools, etc. As we think about our drivers going forward, we do think that there is a third way where we can provide our drivers with minimum wage guarantees and health care to some extent and protections. You know, the laws of the land are one[s] where if you're an employee, you get a bunch of protections. If you're not, you get no protections. And we're completely open to a dialogue of a third way that's befitting this new gig economy as well."[11]

At the time, Khosrowshahi acknowledged that the company does not pay for drivers' medical bills or lost wages if they are victims of sexual assaults that occur during trips enabled by the Uber platform. As of April 2022, Uber was providing subsidies for health care benefits to some drivers in California. But these subsidies were largely mandated by a state measure, Proposition 22, that the company had lobbied against.

Platform companies and other types of organizations face ethical decisions about how and whether to support basic needs for people in their workforce ecosystem. There are difficult ethical choices to make about what is owed—morally—to contingent workers. It is incumbent on organizations that embrace a community-oriented workforce ecosystem to communicate what that actually means in terms of their duty to care for contingent workers. It means little to encourage a sense of belonging among the extended workforce but then undermine that very sense of belonging by denying reasonable protections and benefits. Leaders need to ask whether their respect for contingent workers translates to action on behalf of these workers' (and their families') health and well-being. Are they walking the talk on issues of belonging, respect, and caring?

Law and Ethics in Workforce Ecosystems

Clearly, what organizations owe workers as a matter of law versus ethics is distinct. The former is often a question of compliance: regulations and law determine your options and obligations. The latter can be more strategic, with executive decision-making and trade-offs determining options and obligations. These ethical decisions can be, as Harvard Business School professor Lynn Sharp argues, broader, deeper, and more demanding than a legal or regulatory compliance initiative. Sharp explains, "Broader in that it seeks to enable responsible conduct. Deeper in that it cuts to the ethos and operating systems of the organization and its members, their guiding values and patterns of thought and action. And more demanding in that it requires an active effort to define the responsibilities and aspirations that constitute an organization's ethical compass."[12]

Hilton's ethical compass played a large part in the company's response to the pandemic when it furloughed tens of thousands of hotel staff. By furloughing employees rather than laying them off, the company continued to pay their health benefits. This wasn't entirely altruistic. Hilton wanted its employees to be ready and available to come back to work once the pandemic's effects on travel abated. At the same time, however, Hilton joined with CVS to create an online talent market in which furloughed Hilton employees could seek temporary or longer-term employment with the consumer retailer.

A team of CVS recruiters processed Hilton candidates and identified suitable roles for them within CVS Health.[13] "The recognized quality of our team members, including their hospitality and service culture training, make them ideal candidates to quickly step in and assist organizations in these temporary assignments," said Nigel Glennie, vice president of corporate communication at Hilton, in an interview with *USA Today*. "We hope to expand the program globally, adding more companies, and we plan to welcome these team members back when travel resumes."[14] Hilton helped create opportunities for its furloughed workers. The company wasn't required by law to do this. It wasn't even clearly in its immediate short-term interest. Hilton executives had little idea when or if they would have positions for the furloughed workers, or whether furloughed workers would come back to work for the company. For Hilton and others, supporting these talent markets was an expression of their values and stated principles.

In fact, many companies besides CVS spearheaded talent market initiatives to handle increased demand and take on furloughed workers from other companies, including Amazon, Lidl, Kroger, and Albertsons.[15] More than a hundred companies that had seen depressed demand, like Gap and Marriott, participated in these markets. They expanded their workforce ecosystems, even as their own base of employees contracted. As Jane Oates, former assistant secretary in the US Department of Labor during the Obama administration, said, "It's really a promising practice. This strategy will outlast COVID-19."[16]

Toward a Diverse, Equitable and Inclusive Workforce Ecosystem

Developing and orchestrating an ethical workforce ecosystem can have an outsized impact on how leaders understand and apply DE&I principles. Consider, first, diversity.

Diversity

As companies make the shift to workforce ecosystems, their approach to diversity may change. After all, relying on more contingent workers while retaining diversity goals only for employees encourages a form of diversity whitewashing. That is, touting increases to diversity among the employee base, even as that base becomes a smaller and smaller percentage of workers contributing to value creation, can mislead stakeholders about an organization's performance on its diversity agenda.

This is not an idle concern. Efforts to improve workforce diversity typically focus on employees. A 2021 study of managers in North America found that 71 percent had diversity goals for permanent employees.[17] Few had similar goals for contingent workers, such as service providers offering services under a statement of work (19 percent), temporary workers provided by staffing agencies (16 percent), temporary staffing suppliers (13 percent), gig workers or freelancers (12 percent), and independent contractors (11 percent). Our own 2021 survey shows that only a third of organizations have diversity practices that include external contributors.[18] A diversity agenda that encompasses both employees and external contributors can avoid misleading stakeholders, but that is not yet the common approach.

Misleading stakeholders is, of course, not the only ethical issue concerning diversity in a workforce ecosystem. Let's take a step back and consider why diversity is an ethical matter at all. People are owed respect for their humanity, independently of differences in skin color, ethnicity, gender, age, cognitive functioning, or wealth. Taking diversity seriously means taking each other's humanity seriously.

Diversity is also an ethical matter because it can improve utility. Studies on diversity in organizations demonstrate that having diverse groups of people work together to solve problems and develop opportunities produces better outcomes than less diverse groups of people working together. An oft-cited 2020 McKinsey study finds that businesses with more diverse workforces are more likely to have financial success and deliver higher levels of productivity than those with less diverse workforces.[19] Diversity can help organizations reach their strategic objectives. Thus organizations have at least two ethical reasons to promote diversity: one related to fostering respect and another related to producing good outcomes. Both reasons are essential to any large-scale diversity program.

Diversity can promote opportunity and freedom too. Bosch, the German technology and services company, states that it "values diversity as opportunity and ensures that all associates around the globe feel valued and can freely devote their individual strengths, experience, and potential to the company."[20] Enabling a diverse group of workers to contribute to value creation, for example, may increase access to economic opportunity for those who had yet to enjoy such access. Their new opportunity, their new capability to take advantage of such opportunity, can make a real contribution to social welfare. As Nobel Prize–winning economist and philosopher Amartya Sen wrote in his book *Development as Freedom*, "The freedom to enter markets can itself be a significant contribution to development."[21] Freedom is an ethical benefit, a moral good, as is the ability to pursue opportunity. In a business context, diversity as freedom raises this question: To what extent do diverse workers have the freedom to pursue opportunity at all levels of the organization or across the workforce ecosystem?

Given the ethical nature of diversity, what do leaders need to consider about diversity in an ethical workforce ecosystem? It's important to define what diversity means across your workforce ecosystem. How will you measure diversity? What data is required to do so? Who will be responsible for collecting that data? Will your diversity metrics be tied to any larger set of metrics that matter to executives, such as strategic key performance indicators (KPIs) or objectives and key results (OKRs)? How will you communicate your diversity performance? As companies make the shift to workforce ecosystems, data collection efforts need to expand beyond employee surveys. Aligning your diversity goals with those of other organizations in your workforce ecosystem may require a separate set of measures. You may need to develop a total workforce ecosystem diversity measure. How would that be different than your current diversity goals and measures?

Inclusion

The notion of inclusion is often tied to three concepts: belonging, respect, and feeling valued. In their book *Building an Inclusive*

Organization, Stephen Frost and Raafi-Karim Alidina distinguish inclusion from diversity:

> Only 12% of organizations believe they are inclusive. And even those place too much emphasis on extrinsic factors such as the recruitment pipeline, rather than intrinsic factors such as leadership behavior and culture. In other words, they focus on diversity and representation—getting the right mix of people, with the right skills and competencies. They don't focus enough on inclusion—making sure the mix we have works. *It's about people feeling a sense of belonging, feeling respected, and valued for who they are.*[22]

These three aspects of inclusion—a sense of belonging, feeling respected, and feeling valued—may mean different things to different workers in different organizations. But these differences have a common core for employees. It is a sense of belonging to *their* organization, feeling respected by *their* organization, and feeling valued or accepted by *their* organization. Leaders can clearly articulate what they mean when discussing inclusion for their employees, whether or not the company is good or bad at cultivating it.

Articulating what inclusion means within a workforce ecosystem—both for employees and external contributors—is more complicated. On the one hand, our research suggests that organizations frequently try to extend their code of conduct so that management and others treat *every* worker with respect and embrace differences among individual contributors. Respecting the dignity of persons transcends organizational boundaries and holds to ethical principles expressed by philosopher Immanuel Kant, among others. One of Shell's contractors, Wood, has rhetoric that exemplifies this approach:

> The way we treat the most vulnerable people in our work environment says a great deal about our ethics and culture and whether we really demonstrate our commitment to care. Our itinerant workforce are some of the more silent members of our project teams, often drawn from more vulnerable communities and locations, working sometimes many thousands of miles from home. The way that we care for these team members is equal to and/or greater than any other relationship at the project level, or at least it should be! Maintaining the dignity, fairness, health and welfare of our workforce remains a key priority for our industry especially where there is little or no protection under domestic laws.[23]

On the other hand, as you consider workers further and further out on the periphery of value creation for the enterprise, defining a sense of belonging becomes more difficult. There are at least three complicating factors. One is that external contributors often like their independence; they may not even desire a "sense of belonging" (this can also be true for employees, of course). The rideshare driver who gets irritated by all the prompts from Lyft to participate in its community may prefer Uber's platform, which simply connects drivers with paying customers.

For the company's part, cultivating a sense of belonging among some but not other external contributors is a choice. There is nothing inherently or morally wrong about inviting some rather than others to be a part of your organization's community, so long as their human dignity is respected. Does an invitation to the corporate holiday party reflect your value to the company? Does its absence? In a school setting, everyone is equal, everyone belongs. In a business context, while everyone is equal, everyone may not belong, nor feel that they do. Certainly we've seen organizations—like NASA, for instance—treat external contributors performing mission-critical work over long periods of time as valuable members of their community. But this needn't be the model for all companies. It may be more practical to develop inclusive practices that *welcome* all workers as opposed to trying to create a sense of belonging for all.

The deeper question is, When is it right to include rather than exclude contingent workers? Here we see an ongoing shift. Mike Smith of Randstad Sourceright gives two examples:

> A client of ours wanted to offer our placement and off-boarding services to their contingent workers. If they've done a great job for the first twelve months, we will offer them some type of light off-boarding service. That includes a résumé review [and] access to a learning management microsite. But we want them to walk away going, "Yeah, wow. They really looked after me. They even off-boarded me in a way that no other organization has as a contingent, gig worker, or whatever. And my propensity to want to come back and accept another assignment or a project to work with them with my critical skill set will be higher, as a result of that experience."

Smith describes another situation in which a worker unsuccessfully applies for a contingent job at an organization. To keep the applicant in its workforce ecosystem, the company offers the person access to microskills or other development options in the company's learning management system. The idea here is that the worker has a better chance to fill the position and so does the company.

Action Questions

We have identified several high-level, ethical questions that executives should consider for their workforce ecosystems. Broadly, leaders will likely need to bring together multiple stakeholders to define an ethical approach to addressing all the participants within their workforce ecosystem, whether they work directly for the company (as an employee or contractor), through another company, or as a volunteer. Once having defined this approach, leaders will likely need to create a new system of accountability—with distinct measures, more extensive data collection efforts, and involving new stakeholders.

1. What are leaders' ethical responsibilities toward a workforce that extends beyond (and sometimes far beyond) organizational boundaries?

2. How should leaders make workforce ecosystems fair and inclusive for both internal employees and external contributors?

3. How should leaders support and promote ethical behavior across workforce ecosystems?

11 Implications for Social Responsibility

My concern, when you look at this type of economy, is how do you end up with the appropriate retirement? Or if they're going gig to gig, how do you make sure that they have the right financial security? Are there things you can do that are more portable for employees in terms of benefits so that they have access to what they need at the right time for them?

—Susan Podlogar, MetLife

The notion of social responsibility for companies will become even more important as companies rely more on external workers. There are a lot of people who have had a higher degree of job security and stability with long term employment. So, what if you can fast-forward to a time when more people may no longer have that? How will people cope? What can companies do to continue to live up to expectations?

—Markus Graf, Novartis

For all of their potential to expand economic opportunity and promote wealth creation, workforce ecosystems also have the potential to strain government resources, entrench economic inequalities, and worsen financial, health, and family vulnerabilities, especially among low-wage workers. Concerns about these dark possibilities are not new.[1] They are long-standing, global, and intensifying—and for good reason.

Policy makers and business leaders alike—increasingly and globally—are addressing these concerns. The results so far are uneven. A great deal of work remains to be done.

This chapter describes some of the main challenges that workforce ecosystems pose to workers' social and economic security, along with business's responsibility for the welfare of participants in their workforce ecosystem. We also set the context for this discussion both historically and internationally. Throughout the chapter, we offer questions for executives as they consider how adopting and orchestrating workforce ecosystems will impact their overall corporate purpose and social responsibility. The chief goal of this chapter is to raise and begin to address the following questions:

1. How should leaders think about their social responsibilities for participants within their workforce ecosystem?

2. To what extent does an organization, especially a for-profit business, have responsibility for the economic security of those who move in and out of its workforce ecosystem? Is it enough simply to pay contingent workers for the work they do?

3. Do these choices reflect an organization's social purpose? Does your workforce ecosystem strengthen or weaken the social and economic security of all of those who participate in it?

Historical and International Context

In 1993, well before the dot-com boom and emergence of gig workers, the US government appointed the Commission on the Future of Worker-Management Relations to explore ways to improve workplace productivity, collective bargaining laws, and dispute resolution. The commission was dubbed the Dunlop Commission after its chair, John T. Dunlop, secretary of labor from 1975 to 1976. Its final report found that

> the growth of various forms of contingent work poses opportunities for good job matches between workers with differing labor force attachments and

employers needing flexibility in response to changing market conditions. At the same time, some contingent work arrangements relegate workers to a second-class status of low wages, inadequate fringe benefits, lack of training and, most importantly, loss of protection of labor and employment laws and standards.[2]

Clearly, by the early 1990s, US policy makers had already become concerned about balancing employer flexibility with workers' economic security. The report anticipated that an imbalance would have a negative effect on the country's Social Security system; for instance, business contributions to Social Security were based on employee payroll taxes, which didn't (and still don't) apply to contingent workers.

These US-focused concerns have only grown over time. Brandeis University professor David Weil's 2014 book *The Fissured Workplace* insightfully and rigorously documents the disadvantages that contingent workers, particularly low-wage earners, increasingly face in the US workplace. One poignant story he recounts concerns miners who work for subcontractors. This group of miners is 40 percent more likely to be exposed to fatality risks than those who work as direct employees.[3]

In 2018, researchers at the Urban Institute claimed, "There is growing concern that the safety net is increasingly at odds with current and future labor market realities."[4] For example, US-based contingent workers are not covered by compensation protection laws. Plus, as researchers at Georgetown University's Center for Retirement Initiatives observed, contingent workers often lack access to employer-based retirement plans and typically "don't take action on their own to save if their employer does not provide a plan," compromising their options for a secure retirement.[5]

The effects of higher levels of contingent work on social security are a global concern. The growth of "precarious" work—which can include contingent work—is now common in wealthy democracies such as Germany, Japan, South Korea, Spain, the United Kingdom, and the United States, argues University of Pennsylvania sociologist Arne L. Kalleberg.[6] Precarious work—work that is uncertain, unstable, and insecure, and

confers few, if any, benefits—has always been present in these countries, but its growth in the past three decades has become a concern to
policy makers.[7]

Of course, not all contingent work falls into this category of precarious work. Data scientists and other technology specialists may participate in contingent arrangements for premium prices and benefits. For
many contingent workers, however, the extent of the precariousness
of work arrangements is intimately connected to their lack of power.
In 2017, for instance, contingent workers were three times more likely
than standard full-time workers and nearly five times more likely than
standard part-time workers to be laid off during an economic down-
turn.[8] Recent trends suggest that these numbers will likely increase
without deliberate intervention.

In addition to precarious work, a dearth of good jobs punctuates the
global labor market. The challenge is so severe that providing decent
jobs for youths is now part of the UN Sustainable Development Goals.
Evidence indicates that the great resignation during the pandemic
was due, in part, to a shortage of good jobs.[9] As workforce ecosystems
become more prevalent, will they reduce the incidence and consequences of precarious work? Will they generate good jobs that provide
economic security as well as meaningful opportunities?

Addressing the Challenges

Both policy makers and businesses are beginning to address these challenges. The International Labour Organization has adopted a decent
work agenda "to deliver quality jobs along with social protection and
respect for rights at work to achieve sustainable, inclusive economic
growth, and eliminate poverty."[10] In 2000, the Council of the European
Union, meeting in Lisbon, agreed on an ambitious goal "to become
the most competitive and dynamic knowledge-based economy in the
world, capable of sustainable economic growth with more and better
jobs and greater social cohesion."[11] This became known as the Lisbon
Strategy or the "more, better jobs" strategy.

The European policy of Flexicurity, which aims to advance the Lisbon Strategy agenda, explicitly acknowledges the need to strengthen legal protections for workers, support lifelong learning, and improve welfare protection systems. These protections are not just for shocks and retirement. They also embrace what our coauthor Jeff Schwartz calls "transition nets," which support workers as they transition in and out of jobs, in and out of employment, during longer work lives.[12]

Some businesses are stepping up. More companies are explicitly making a point of providing living wages across their workforce ecosystems (such as Unilever and Bank of America, to cite two) along with offering training and learning opportunities as well as access to pension-planning tools for contingent workers.[13]

Progress is clearly uneven. More jobs and upskilling haven't translated into broad improvements in job quality.[14] Compliance with laws that are specifically designed to support economic security, such as pay parity and equal pay for equal work regulations, remains a work in progress. Proposed worker classification laws that could enable millions of platform-based workers to become employees with benefits continue to be debated or resisted by business.

Many companies claim that employees are their greatest asset, they prize inclusion, and taking care of their employees is central to their organizational purpose. But once leaders find that their organizations have become highly dependent on external workers, they ought to question whether their social responsibilities should shift as well. They may need to ask such questions as the following: Is the economic security of all people who generate value for our company our concern, whether or not they are *our* employees? If the economic security of some but not all people who generate value for our company is our concern, where should we draw the line? Is it at providing a living wage for everyone in our workforce ecosystem? Does everyone get access to learning opportunities and other benefits? What principles of fairness should we apply to these questions?[15] These are difficult questions with a wide range of legitimate responses. First and foremost, leaders need to believe that these questions are worth asking.

Strengthening Economic Security

> The realization came that we have responsibility for the inner and the outer core of employees. If you want to change the world, if you want to live your social commitments, if you want to make sure that you always have a skilled workforce, inside and outside of your company, you systemically need to change that whole chain that you are responsible for.
>
> —Jeroen Wels, Unilever (former)

Taking responsibility for the economic security of people who move in and out of your workforce ecosystem is easier said than done, especially since this notion goes beyond pay to include needs such as food, basic shelter, clothing, health care, and hygiene.

The International Community of the Red Cross defines economic security as the ability of individuals, households, or communities to cover their essential needs sustainably and with dignity.[16] This goes beyond the scope of issues that employers, particularly those with locations primarily in the United States, have traditionally dealt with, and indeed it can be easier to avoid responsibility altogether. Today, we see economic security issues playing out in the current battle over whether Uber and Lyft drivers along with other platform workers are employees. But the battle for employee status and the benefits that status tends to bring is not new.

Consider the plight of 180,000 home care workers in California who wanted to join the Service Employees International Union (SEIU) in the 1980s. To join the union, these workers needed an employer of record; after all, the SEIU is a union of and for employees. Initially, the home care workers assumed their employer was California, which gave them their paychecks each week. But as one observer noted, "The State said, 'not us, perhaps the County.' So, the homecare workers looked to the County, which assigned them to clients and set their hours. The County said, 'not us, perhaps the clients themselves.'"[17]

Litigation followed, with no entity willing to admit to being their employer. Not without reason: the home care workers' compensation came from a blend of federal, state, and county funds, making it difficult to single out a sole employer. The California Supreme Court decided that the home care workers were independent contractors who worked for their individual clients. In response, the SEIU persuaded the state legislature to pass a law in 1992 that authorized counties to create authorities that would administer the home care programs and serve as the workers' employers. The SEIU worked across the state to get counties to establish such authorities. By 1999, tens of thousands of California-based home workers had joined the SEIU. In some cases, the benefits came quickly. For instance, after San Francisco's home care workers joined the union, they received a contract that raised their hourly wage from \$5.75 to \$7, and also provided health insurance.[18]

It's clear that issues around classifying workers with ambiguous or complex ties to an organization have a long history. The Dunlop Commission report's recommendations on this point are instructive. It recommended that the federal government adopt

> a single definition of employee for all workplace laws based on the economic realities of the employment relationship. The law should confer independent contractor status only on those for whom it is appropriate—entrepreneurs who bear the risk of loss, serve multiple clients, hold themselves out to the public as an independent business, and so forth. The law should not provide incentives for misclassification of employees as independent contractors, which costs federal and state treasuries large sums in uncollected social security, unemployment, personal income, and other taxes.[19]

Long before the advent of e-commerce, gig workers, and trillion-dollar platform companies, the Dunlop Commission's recommendations—most of which were not adopted—described significant concerns about the effects of extended workforces.[20]

With the emergence of platform-based companies, worker classification laws have significant implications for both businesses and workers, influencing the prospects of millions of workers. In 2021, the European Commission proposed a law that would, if passed by European Union members, radically change how digital platforms like Uber and Lyft operate in the European Union.[21] The law—an expression of "flexicurity" principles—would directly affect the treatment of tens of millions of EU workers.[22] It creates a presumption that a platform worker is an employee, but offers platform companies an opportunity to challenge this presumption. Under the proposed law, if any two of the following five factors apply, an individual is presumed to be in an employment relationship with the platform:

1. The platform controls pay
2. The platform sets binding work rules governing how work is done, conduct toward the end user of the services, or the worker's appearance
3. The platform supervises the work done or verifies the quality of work (including by electronic means)
4. The platform exercises control, including through sanctions, over working hours (including the ability to subcontract work or use a substitute, and the ability to accept or refuse particular tasks)
5. The platform restricts or controls the individual's ability to build their own client base or work for another person (such as another digital labor platform)[23]

These new regulations for classifying workers are specifically designed to support workers' economic security. They recognize that workforce ecosystems can have large-scale effects on social and economic arrangements. Policy makers acknowledge that the proposed law would have an effect on platform business models, but they're also trying to find the right way to balance flexible work arrangements with workers' economic security. The law reflects a specific point of view about how the government wants platform companies to assume responsibility for workers' economic security.

Equal Pay for Equal Work

Worker classification laws are just one example of government efforts to ensure that markets balance flexibility and security. Equal pay for equal work laws are another instance. More than thirty countries now have some form of pay parity laws that make companies legally responsible for paying employees and contingent workers similarly for comparable work.[24] Under these laws, it's the work that counts, not the employment status. These laws aren't merely about pay equity; they reflect efforts to combat threats to long-term social welfare, including income inequality and diminished business contributions to welfare protections.

It can be difficult for a company to fully embrace its role in this tug-of-war between flexibility and security. The *New York Times* reported that in December 2020, Google managers discovered that compensation for many contingent workers was out of compliance with pay parity laws in certain countries.[25] The company faced a dilemma. On the one hand, if it corrected the error, it would quickly become public that Google had been out of compliance. This was a politically sensitive issue given that the US Congress had told the company just a year or so before to improve its treatment of temps and contractors. On the other hand, if it did not correct the error, it would knowingly be noncompliant, putting managers and the company in legal jeopardy. Senior managers found a middle ground. They decided to adjust new compensation for new contracts to rectify the error going forward, but not to address existing pay discrepancies. This decision ultimately became public. The company had to issue apologies and renew its commitment to improve its ways.

While equal pay for equal work laws make pay parity into a compliance issue, pay transparency initiatives may transform pay parity into a cultural issue. Daniel Rock, assistant professor of operations, information, and decisions at the Wharton School at the University of Pennsylvania, notes that companies do not want "employees internal to the firm to feel uncomfortable when there are multiple layers of treatment. They don't want tiered systems where internal employees get the benefits of working for the firm and outside contractors don't. In addition to generating fairness concerns, that creates cognitive dissonance that's challenging and costly to manage."[26] Building a strong and inclusive organizational culture can be a reason to promote fair treatment (including compensation equity) across organizational boundaries.

Boosting Benefits

There are practical solutions that companies can embrace now that can help the short-term economic security of contributors to their workforce ecosystems. These solutions can enhance a company's talent brand at minimal cost and simultaneously support social welfare protections. For example, fintech start-ups like DailyPay are helping companies give workers access to earned wages without having to wait weeks or months for payroll systems to process invoices, or biweekly or monthly paychecks. Even.com offers planning, budgeting, and automatic savings tools. Betterment.com offers robo-advising for retirement savings. These tools can boost short-term economic security in unexpected ways.

At DailyPay, executives learned that workers got a lot out of seeing their earned wages in real time. Jeanniey Walden, DailyPay's chief innovation and marketing officer, observed:

> We find that employees are checking their pay balance, which is the number that shows how much they've earned to date, up to six times a day. They start a shift, maybe at a Kroger in the morning, and they're working for a few hours, and then they log in to DailyPay and they see, "Hey, I just worked three hours. It was a Sunday so I got time and a half. Look at how much I've earned. This is great. Now I can start thinking about saving for holiday gifts for the family." Then at the end of the day, they might log in to say, "OK, this is how much money I made today. Do I need to pick up an extra shift? Do I want to pick up an extra shift just so I can have additional funds so I can do things like accelerate my training within a certain ecosystem?" Eighty-seven percent of people who use our app apply for a specific amount of money.

These fintech companies report that access to these tools and benefits improves worker satisfaction along with the brand reputation of employers, which in turn improves participants' experiences within workforce ecosystems.

Lifelong Learning and Reemployment

Workers' aspirations for mobility and meaningful work are growing as they live longer and have more varied careers—a trend summarized well in two recent books: Lynda Gratton and Andrew Scott's *The 100-Year Life: Living and Working in an Age of Longevity*, and Stephen Johnson's *Extra Life: A Short History of Living Longer*.[27] The changing nature of work, diminishing half-life of worker skills, and need to support reemployment as people live and work longer: these social trends all point to a need for a new system of adult education, training, skills development, and credentialing. No wonder corporate education is now a $360 billion global market and growing by nearly 8 percent per year.[28]

Maintaining the refresh rate on skills isn't just a business concern; governments have a vested interest in ensuring that employment levels stay high and that workers can efficiently move from position to position throughout their careers. Sustained employment lulls mean lower revenues with which to fund social programs, which are even more necessary when unemployment levels are high. Financing these programs through debt becomes more likely, as we saw during the recent pandemic, and is an unsustainable approach.

The rise of workforce ecosystems offers a powerful alignment mechanism for business and government to jointly maintain employment levels, develop necessary skills, and fund social programs. The tacit compact between business and government for welfare protections is shifting. As Kalleberg remarks, there is "a reconfiguring of the relationships . . . between public and private providers of social welfare protection."[29] Learning and reskilling is one area where business and government can themselves learn to become more effective partners. Workforce ecosystems can affect the social and political contexts in which they exist, and vice versa.

Governments can do more to support adult reskilling—in the United States, investments in early to postsecondary education ($180 billion) far outpace investments in worker retraining and skills development ($12 billion). A small but growing number of countries, such as Costa

Rica and Morocco, are partnering with online learning platforms like Coursera to offer adult learning and development courses that can lead to credentials valued by businesses operating in their respective nations. Coursera has created fifteen entry-level professional certifications for entry-level digital jobs in IT support, data science, and bookkeeping, among other roles. These certifications are designed for people without a college degree and with no prior experience in the field. They can be obtained entirely through online coursework. Public-private partnerships can support individual growth and access to opportunity, improve the quality of labor pools, and more broadly, enrich the socioeconomic contexts in which workforce ecosystems operate.

Business leaders can do more to create entry paths into their workforce ecosystems based on these and similar credentials. We saw in chapter 7 that businesses are becoming much more proactive in the upskilling and credentialing markets. In some fast-moving industries, such as the cloud-based computing market, industry players like Microsoft, Nvidia, AWS, and Cisco are not waiting for other companies to develop learning courses. Coursera CEO Jeff Maggioncalda told us that "cloud companies [like Microsoft and Cisco] are creating new capabilities so fast that trainers can't keep up. They have stepped in to create both training materials and certifications." Their efforts are not simply self-serving. As Maggioncalda remarked, "They recognize that their technologies will be automating many jobs, and they are providing training to create greater access to the new jobs their technologies are creating."

Rethinking Corporate Social Responsibility

Taking responsibility for the welfare of both employees and the extended workforce encompasses issues that connect directly to a company's overall purpose and culture, and indirectly to welfare protections for workers' short- and long-term social and economic security.

Leaders are beginning to question whether they can be socially responsible corporate citizens without supporting economic security and welfare throughout their workforce ecosystems. Actions like those of Unilever, Novartis, and others mentioned throughout this book raise an important question for leaders to consider: To what extent should their organization concern itself with the economic security of all the participants in their workforce ecosystem? The process of gaining consensus on the meaning of "concern," "economic security," and "purpose" may prove to be more valuable than any specific answer to this question.

We suggest these questions below to prompt management discussions about how best to approach social responsibility in a workforce ecosystem.

Action Questions

As you answer these, consider an organization where you work or that you would like to analyze.

1. Does the business make an explicit connection between its organizational purpose and the treatment of all the participants in its workforce ecosystem?

2. Are the leaders considering the need for a living wage and access to essential health, family, and retirement resources across the workforce ecosystem?

   ◦ Is paying a livable wage simply good for business—part of the strategy for attracting the best talent—or is it an expression of a more deeply held set of values?

   ◦ What burdens are individuals being asked to shoulder?

   ◦ Is the business and its leadership supporting public services to augment and fill the gaps?

3. In what ways does the organization's workforce ecosystem support and detract from the economic security of all the participants in the extended workforce?

   ◦ How should leaders address the economic security of workers in the workforce ecosystem?

   ◦ What responsibility does the organization have for advancing the economic security of the extended workforce?

4. Should leaders rethink their approach to benefits to align with a work-force ecosystem approach?

5. To what extent should all the members of a workforce ecosystem have access to a company's learning management systems?

- Is this business a learning organization?

- Is the workforce ecosystem a system of learning? Should it be?

Workforce ecosystems require a new approach to managing today's complex, highly interconnected extended workforces. They encompass what we refer to as people, partners, and technologies, including part- and full-time employees; external participants such as long-term contractors, gig workers, professional service providers, subcontractors, and complementors; and even technologies. Workforce ecosystems represent a much more expansive view of workforces than more traditional employee-centric models. They offer new opportunities for organizations to reach strategic goals as they include more diverse contributors of various forms. Still, as we have seen, they present challenges, as managing these far-reaching, dynamic structures elicits new tensions within organizations and between ecosystem participants. While in the past leaders were tasked with managing mostly internal workforces, today they find themselves having to orchestrate wide-ranging workforce ecosystems.

The ongoing transition from managing workforces to orchestrating workforce ecosystems is a continuing struggle. In this book we have covered the basics of workforce ecosystems, and delved more deeply into areas that our research reveals are most important for leaders and managers. We have explored these topics primarily through the lens of leaders and managers as they need to reckon with workforce ecosystems if they are to be successful over time. We recognize that we have not yet fully accounted for the perspective of individual actors in workforce ecosystems. While worker perspectives may certainly be useful to understanding workforce ecosystems, their views tend to vary by industry, geography, demography, skill level, and employment status. Unfortunately, a full treatment of this subject lies beyond the scope of this book.

We are well aware that the workforce ecosystem framework we propose may help entrench a troubling "fissuring" of the workplace that distributes work-related risks and responsibilities to third parties, individuals, and governments.[1] But throughout our research, we have found well-intentioned leaders focused on taking greater responsibility for a broader group of workers and workforce ecosystem contributors. We are heartened to see that senior executives in a variety of organizations are recognizing the need to consider the consequences of shifting workforce boundaries and composition: moreover, they are taking action. In many of our conversations, leaders have embraced the workforce ecosystem framework as a way to not only better manage their business but also for their company to contribute more to society.

That said, norms are still in flux and being created. We have identified the management practices worth emulating and the questions leaders need to be asking themselves in order to equitably orchestrate an inclusive workforce ecosystem.

It is not too early to anticipate how workforce ecosystems will inspire new management practices. Toward that end, this closing chapter has three sections. The first one discusses several potential management practice innovations. The second touches on the need for businesses and governments to work together to address the societal implications of workforce ecosystems. Finally, the third section explores the need for a new type of leadership mindset to successfully orchestrate workforce ecosystems.

New Management Practices

Workforce Ecosystem Analysis
As workforce ecosystems become more established as structures requiring orchestration, the analysis of workforce ecosystems will likely

become a management subdiscipline—perhaps one that combines people analytics, behavioral economics, organizational network analysis, and data visualization. The evolution of workforce ecosystem analytics will make it easier for companies to visualize and manage workforce ecosystems.

We imagine some intriguing developments in this area. For example, one is the more extensive integration of AI into tools that make predictions for staffing requirements, or help workers find positions within companies or workforce ecosystems. Another area is the visualization of the supply and demand of skills. Visualizing the workforce ecosystem structure would involve mapping the existing supply of workforce streams, skills deployments, and inventory, and predicting where the demand is expected to be. These analytics would also surface interdependencies, complementors, and the range of actors who have and might contribute value. The information demands for achieving these visualizations are nontrivial, but they are possible without breaking the bank. Think digital twins for your total workforce. The ability to map your workforce ecosystem can play a valuable role when devising strategy, such as clarifying whether a particular strategy is too costly or even practical given its labor and resource demands.

It would be an incomplete use of analytics, however, if workforce ecosystem structure analysis centered only on skills. Workforce ecosystem structure analytics also have the potential to shed light on progress toward DE&I goals and the economic security of contributors throughout the workforce ecosystem.

What's more, workforce ecosystem analytics could reveal how human capital flows through and among multiple workforce ecosystems. We have continued to recognize connections between workforce ecosystems that cross industry boundaries. For example, staffing agencies—which interact with multiple workforce ecosystems—could play a critical role in providing competitors with benchmarking information about talent mobility, credentialing, time to hire, DE&I, and salaries across workforce ecosystems. The global staffing industry has grown to just below five hundred billion dollars in revenues (2019), with staffing agencies generating 75 percent of this number.[2] To be sure, some companies, like Toptal, Catalant, and Experfy, are developing platforms that connect external contributors directly with businesses, thus disintermediating staffing agencies. But a robust workforce ecosystem analytics platform would incorporate their data as well.

New Outcome Measures

The continued development of workforce ecosystems may alter how companies define and use outcome measures. As MetLife's Susan Podlogar told us, "Once we understand the skills needed, and take steps to unlock the potential of the organization in new ways, we are playing for a bigger outcome than productivity." Consider a commonly used HR metric, *revenue per employee* (or the less politically acceptable label, *return on employee*). This ratio of total revenues divided by the average number of employees is deemed by some to be among the most important business and HR metrics.[3] But what should we do with this revenue per employee metric if external contributors are responsible for 30 to 50 percent of the financial results? In that case, revenue per employee provides a partial and perhaps misleading view of how employees contribute to financial success. Discussions get even more complicated when we factor in technology investments that augment worker performance. These work technologies (discussed in chapter 7) may have a direct effect on an employee's ability to contribute to revenues. Assuming it's even possible to measure that direct effect, is the return on these technologies a return on technology or people, or both? To complicate matters even further, the rise of human-machine interactions is blurring traditional divides between capital- and labor-intensive businesses, raising important questions about how to measure performance drivers.

These shifts portend novel techniques for measuring performance and new metrics. We may see revenue per contributor metrics that offer nuanced views about how to attribute revenues, indifferent to whether a contributor is a person, partner, or technology. We may also see the development and acceptance of "good jobs" measures that show the extent to which a workforce ecosystem is producing (and filling) good jobs as they are now variously defined.

The European Job Quality Index offers both precedent and a template for such measures. It assesses jobs in six dimensions: wages; forms of employment and job security; working time and work-life balance; working conditions; skills and career development; and collective interest representation.[4] Many other organizations have developed some form of a job quality or good jobs index, including but certainly not limited to the Organisation for Economic Co-operation and Development, Bill and Melinda Gates Foundation, Gallup, and Georgetown with JP Morgan Chase.[5] Most of these indexes and measures apply to sectors, states, countries, or regions. The next step is for companies to develop and apply their own good jobs indexes within their own workforce ecosystems.

Vigorous debates about how to measure productivity and define other outcome benchmarks will help companies better understand their business.

The Changing Role of Managers and Team Leaders

A theme of this book is the role of workforce ecosystems as a new structure for relationships among workers and all types of contributors—inside and outside the organization—and business leaders at all levels. Workforce ecosystems are connected through relationships, culture, the alignment of shared values, and the contribution to personal and collective value. From one perspective, it is the relationships that structure a workforce ecosystem, and as such the role of line managers and team leaders is critical to its success and impact.

As organizations embrace the need to manage workforce ecosystem structures, we expect that management training, measurement, and rewards will change. Workforce ecosystems—combined with the changing nature of physical, hybrid, and remote work; new combinations of human-machine teams; and the pervasive role of digital technologies—will combine to create new development opportunities for managers. For example, managers may be recognized or otherwise supported for help-ing high-value talent transfer to other departments—talent they might have otherwise "hoarded" in a more siloed work environment. The workers may be offered opportunities for short-term assignments with ecosystem partners such as subcontractors or professional services firms.

From Acquisition and Attrition to Access and Attraction

We believe that attrition will get less scary as workforce ecosystems gain traction in the marketplace. That may sound overly optimistic. And it may be in the short-term. But if we take seriously the idea that well-orchestrated workforce ecosystems will be able to supply the right people at the right time for the right work, then the risks of attrition do become less scary, in two senses in particular.

In one sense, attrition becomes less scary because it becomes less of a risk. As we discussed earlier, talent marketplaces can improve both talent mobility and retention. Creating talent markets with good jobs—accessible to both internal employees and external contributors—ensures a steady flow of talent within and across organizational boundaries. Credentials, badges, and other verifiable skills-signaling mechanisms that have an inherent or distinctive value within a com-pany's workforce ecosystem will expand timely access to the right tal-ent. Improved technology systems will track where skilled workers are within the ecosystem and predict demand. Putting specialized external contributors on retainer may become a preferred contractual relation-ship for both employers and contributors.

In another sense, attrition becomes less scary because it is easier to address at a lower cost. Today, the costs of replacing an employee—from search to onboarding—are high and continuing to rise. In future workforce ecosystems, an employee who decides to leave a company's workforce ecosystem creates several opportunities. One is the oppor-tunity to reassess whether the person's role could or should be decom-posed into groups of tasks for others to do. This needn't add more work to other people's existing roles; it may be possible to use talent markets to find other skilled workers interested in taking on these tasks. This is not a new activity, of course, but with future workforce ecosystems, organizations will be able to take a much more proactive, and even pre-emptive, approach that will be improved through insights on how to access replacement skills among employees and external contributors.

For instance, most companies make succession planning a to-do for high-level positions, but it's now possible (or soon will be) for companies to make succession planning a more pervasive phenomenon for a wider range of positions and tasks. If the half-life of skills in a given position is decreasing, employee loyalty is on the decline, and the average tenure of a worker is dropping, these are strong reasons to expand succession planning efforts. With improved insights on where and how to access skills in the workforce ecosystem, the search costs for new talent, including time to hire, may drop. The search costs would drop further with larger investments in building a talent pool to back up employees in existing roles. Succession planning need not be hidden from workers; done properly, it could be an opportunity to engage employees about where they would like to go next in the organization or elsewhere, and help those in their personal network who might be suitable replacements. Including employees in the succession planning process could reveal their personal networks, which could lower the costs of replacing workers. For the skeptics, employees have a genuine self-interest in supporting their own succession if the benefits of doing so are clearly articulated.

Public Policy and Institutions

The preponderance of employment and educational policy is based on the concepts of twentieth century (and earlier) labor and business models. These were predicated on operational scale, stability, and physical colocation, and the idea that careers were "one and done": you studied a trade, worked for an organization for twenty-five to thirty years, and retired. US tax and Social Security policies have largely been based on discrete, identifiable employment categories. In a world of multiple employment models with most workers having careers that weave across different employment contracts, more sophisticated policy, tax, and educational programs will be required.

We are at a critical juncture in the relationship between business and government. The emergence of workforce ecosystems is imposing new pressures and costs on social safety nets. Across industries and geographies, companies vary widely in their willingness to embrace responsibility for contributors in their workforce ecosystems. Good jobs remain in short supply. Trust in business and government are at historic lows in many countries. Plus, many trends are influencing the dynamics between business and government, including general AI, automation, quantum computing, embedded and wearable technologies, climate change, demographic shifts, civic unrest, hybrid work, the Internet of Things, the metaverse, robots, and advanced renewables.

This context is important to bear in mind as workforce ecosystems are increasingly recognized not only as structures to be orchestrated but also potentially regulated. Already, some have proposed policies that require leading companies to absorb the social costs of shedding traditional employment responsibilities.[6] The right mix of regulatory incentives and self-regulation is not yet clear, especially for companies operating in multiple jurisdictions.

The emergence of workforce ecosystems brings legitimate concerns. But we see many leaders taking their responsibilities seriously. There are clear signs that workforce ecosystems can expand access to work and educational opportunities in both developed and emerging economies. They can support a new era of value creation for business and society alike. Or not. This is a choice. Yet it is not a choice for business or government alone. Business and government need to work together, while keeping the interests of workers and consumers front and center.

A Workforce Ecosystem Mindset

Leaders have experienced multiple technologically driven shifts and transformations over recent decades enabled by enterprise computing, mobile technologies, cloud services, machine learning, AI, blockchain, and others. Still, though some of these shifts have had extensive implications, they have not yet affected workforce-related challenges in meaningful and wide-ranging ways. This is true in large, mature organizations as well as smaller enterprises. Though the technologies exist to allow them, by and large, few companies have yet been formed relying natively on workforce ecosystems. Thus in the same way that many leaders are digital immigrants working to understand how best to leverage quickly evolving technologies, most executives are workforce ecosystem immigrants too. This requires leaders to adopt a new mindset geared more specifically toward the opportunities and challenges presented by workforce ecosystems.

Adding to this challenge, workforce ecosystems often do not operate as stand-alone systems. They tend to be sprawling and have various connections with other workforce ecosystems. Some workforce ecosystems are nested within larger ones, and others may connect through customers or suppliers either in the same industry or across industries— essentially operating as chains of workforce ecosystems. Earlier in the book, we saw companies like CVS and Kroger creating cross-industry talent markets that absorbed workers with needed skills from the hospitality (Marriott and Hilton) and retail (Gap Inc.) sectors.

In the future, organizations may find that orchestrating their workforce ecosystems in conjunction with other workforce ecosystems can help manage the flow of talent and contributors in and out of their workforce, not just during crises, but on an ongoing basis. Again, leaders need to ensure that they and their teams are updating their thinking to consider the various permutations of connected workforce ecosystems, with the interdependencies and complementarities that these relationships may bring.

Adopting a workforce ecosystem mindset and coordinating potentially across workforce ecosystems may take several forms:

1. Leaders may shift what are often single company-centric mindsets to a more expansive view that considers not only their own workforce ecosystems but also building relationships with other workforce ecosystems. This could enable them to attract more talent and/or

appeal to a larger array of complementors with similar capabilities. They could showcase opportunities and success stories that emerge across multiple workforce ecosystems. These groups of workforce ecosystems could present opportunities and benefits to universities and developer communities, for example, supplementing and complementing corporate outreach to these institutions. These groups could highlight the many opportunities in essentially a community of workforce ecosystems.

2. Managers could think beyond individual company-based credentialing to collaborate with other organizations to create proprietary credentialing systems that deliver a distinctive meaning and value to organizations within a given association. For workers, these credentials might be more valuable than a credential from a single company; such credentials would offer more options and mobility, and decrease the risk that a credential valued by a single company would become less valuable over time.

3. Competitors may expand their thinking to work together aligning their workforce ecosystems. For instance, German carmakers (Mercedes, Audi, and BMW) formed an alliance with Intel to acquire the mapping division HERE from Nokia. While retaining specialized manufacturing, sales, and engineering talent is clearly important to each carmaker in this alliance, each company also has demand for similar skills that may be in short supply (e.g., data science). What traditionally may have been pursued either as single or multiparty alliances among competitors may become workforce ecosystem alliances when the benefits of collectively accessing talent and contributor communities outweigh the costs of competing for talent. These alliances may be especially attractive in situations where there are talent shortfalls or expected skills deficits. In such alliances, corporate leaders and their stakeholders will need to closely monitor pay equity to ensure fair wages across the ecosystem.

By using an ecosystem lens to view today's more expansive and interconnected extended workforces, leaders are able to capture not only that these workforces include many types of participants engaged through various business arrangements but also that they have complex relationships between them. Workforce ecosystem members are interdependent on each other, have individual and joint strategic goals, and frequently have complementarities even if they are not contractually working together.

In closing, workforce ecosystems offer leaders new opportunities to develop new management practices for new outcomes. A workforce ecosystems perspective allows leaders to take a much richer and more nuanced view of organizations along with the people, partners, and technologies on which they rely to capture and create value. As leaders consider how to reach bold strategic goals, workforce ecosystems offer the ability to effectively work with people, partners, and technologies in innovative and effective ways. Orchestrating workforce ecosystems provides a new way to create new strategic visions and bring them to reality.

Appendix A: List of Interviewees with Affiliations

First name	Last name	Organization
Elizabeth	Adefioye	Emerson
Kevin	Akeroyd	PRO Unlimited
Jennifer	Arcuni	Versal
Milford H.	Beagle Jr.	US Army
Cathy	Benko	board member (NIKE, Inc., SolarWinds, and WorkBoard)
Josh	Bersin	HR industry analyst
Ty	Breland	Marriott International
Cynthia	Bullock	Virginia Department of Transportation
Jacqui	Canney	ServiceNow
Oren	Cass	American Compass
Carmelo	Cennamo	Copenhagen Business School
Tomas	Chamorro-Premuzic	ManpowerGroup
Ronald P.	Clark	US Army
Kori	Covrigaru	PlanOmatic
Roland	Deiser	Drucker School of Management at Claremont Graduate University
Julie	Derene	Ceridian
Tony	DiRomualdo	The Hackett Group
Taso	Du Val	Toptal
Paul	Estes	XpertLinkAI
Jennifer	Felch	Dell Technologies
Dyan	Finkhousen	Open Assembly
Diane	Gherson	Harvard Business School
Robert	Gibbs	NASA

First name	Last name	Organization
Ankur	Gopal	Interapt
Markus	Graf	Novartis
Dror	Gurevich	Velocity Network Foundation
Doug	Haaland	Whirlpool Corporation
Hannah	Hennig	Siemens AG
Thomas	Kochan	MIT Sloan School of Management
Tobias	Kretschmer	Ludwig-Maximilians-Universität München
Martin	Krzywdzinski	Helmut Schmidt Universität - Universität der Bundeswehr Hamburg
Mary	Lacity	University of Arkansas
Nickle	LaMoreaux	IBM
Paul	LeBlanc	Southern New Hampshire University
Jeff	Maggioncalda	Coursera
Barbry	McGann	Workday Ventures
Donna	Morris	Walmart
Jared	Mueller	Mayo Clinic
Susan	Podlogar	MetLife
Jill	Popelka	SAP SuccessFactors
Catherine	Popper	Launchpad Venture Group
Doron	Reuveni	Applause
Daniel	Rock	Wharton School at the University of Pennsylvania
Andrew	Saidy	Ubisoft
Chandra	Sanders	The Mom Project
Nicholas	Skytland	NASA
Mike	Smith	Randstad Sourceright
Arun	Srinivasan	Banyan Software
Susan	Tincher	University of Southern California
Susan	Tohyama	Ceridian
Alan	Trefler	Pegasystems
Christopher	Tucci	Imperial College London
Dave	Ulrich	University of Michigan
Jeanniey	Walden	DailyPay
Katia	Walsh	Levi Strauss & Co.

First name	Last name	Organization
Jane	Weinmann	Roche
Meredith	Wellard	Deutsche Post DHL Group
Jeroen	Wels	Unilever (former)
David	Wengel	iDatafy
Cristina A.	Wilbur	Roche
Jeff	Wilke	Re:Build Manufacturing
Ying	Yuan Ng	DBS Bank

Note: This list includes many people (and their organizations) who we do not explicitly quote in this book, but who we did interview as part of our multi-year research project. We acknowledge them all here because each of them helped us to advance our thinking about the subjects covered in this book. Please note that we interviewed other experts in the field also as part of this research but were not able to list them all.

Appendix B: Survey and Interview Data Collection Research Methodology

In fall 2019, we conducted our ninth annual survey including nearly thirty-nine hundred business executives, managers, and analysts. We explored perspectives about evolving relationships between organizations and workers, especially focused on trends *within* the organization and changes related to managing the employee base. The worldwide, cross-industry survey captured insights from individuals in 126 countries and 28 industries at organizations of various sizes. More than two-thirds of the respondents were outside the United States. The sample was drawn from sources including *MIT Sloan Management Review* readers, Deloitte Dbriefs webcast subscribers, and other parties. In addition to administering a survey, we interviewed leaders and executives from industry and academia to understand how organizations invest in their workforces today. In some cases, executives were spearheading novel approaches to workforce investment and managing workers in a digital age. A number of executives came from HR, but many did not, enabling us to gain a holistic view across functional areas.

In fall 2020, *MIT Sloan Management Review* and Deloitte built on the prior year's research by choosing to not only examine changes within organizations but also more explicitly address workforce shifts in organizations that were engaging with external contributors beyond their traditional employee bases. We surveyed over five thousand individuals from around the world to better understand how they approach strategic workforce management issues. Respondents represented 114 countries, more than 29 industries, and organizations of various sizes.

More than two-thirds of the respondents were from outside the United States, and over 30 percent had personally worked in a contingent (nonpermanent) capacity in the past five years. We drew the sample from sources including *MIT Sloan Management Review* readers, Deloitte's network of executives, and other interested parties. Additionally, the research team conducted twenty-four comprehensive interviews of C-suite executives and other senior leaders from private industry, the public sector, higher education, and the military to explore topics such as shifts in perceptions related to workforces; links between these shifts and organizational strategy and culture; and the implications for management practices. Finally, the team analyzed the management and strategy research literature on ecosystem dynamics, frameworks, and governance structures.

In fall 2021, we launched another global survey, yielding over four thousand responses. We also embarked on another set of interviews with thought leaders in industry, academia, and the nonprofit sector. By this time, we had developed the workforce ecosystem structure and were starting to develop frameworks associated with orchestrating workforce ecosystems as we dug more deeply into how this new structure was affecting management practices. Thus during this survey and interview research, we asked the respondents more specific questions about how they were addressing management practice shifts. Our results provided insights that let us derive the frameworks and recommendations in this book.

The research starting in early 2020 and through 2022 was conducted during the COVID-19 global pandemic, when survey and interview respondents were living through dramatic shifts and evolving transitions in workforce practices. Our survey data and interview responses suggest that many trends driving workforce ecosystems were underway before the pandemic began, and are likely to continue after the most extreme effects of the pandemic subside. Still, we recognize that some trends were likely accelerated during the research and others may have been dampened. It remains to be seen what the trajectory of these trends will be in future years.

Acknowledgments

We've been working on this research for a few years. We have the data. We have published reports and articles on this topic. How hard could it possibly be to pull together a book?

As it turns out, pretty hard. Even when its foundation is an ongoing research project, writing a full-length book takes extraordinary effort and cooperation by more people than one might imagine. (In essence, it takes a workforce ecosystem.)

The four of us feel extremely grateful not only to have found each other but also to have the great fortune of being surrounded by brilliant, committed collaborators. Although we are able to list only a few here, many others have influenced and contributed to our work. Please know that if you had any hand in helping us generate and think through the ideas in this book, or in working with us to bring them to life, we appreciate you and are grateful for all of your contributions. Still, there are a few people we would like to explicitly thank.

Thank you to Emily Taber, Deborah Cantor-Adams, Laura Keeler, Cindy Milstein, and the entire MIT Press team for your confidence in us and for all of your work shepherding this book from proposal through publication. From start to finish, your competence and professionalism has shone through. You have been a pleasure to work with and represent the best in the publishing world.

With the beautiful writing and meticulous editing help of Barbara Spindel, this book is much clearer and easier to read. Her efforts and counsel certainly made it easier for us to write. Thank you, Barbara. We could not have done this without you.

The research that informed the basis of this book is part of the Big Ideas Initiative, Future of the Workforce project (sponsored by Deloitte) at *MIT Sloan Management Review (MIT SMR)*. A portion of the findings we present were originally published in *MIT SMR* through research reports and articles. At *MIT SMR*, Allison Ryder is a standout collaborator who has brought invaluable insights and organization to all of our research efforts. Others from *MIT SMR* who we thank include Cheryl Asselin, Michael Barrette, Deb Gallagher, Bob Holland, Abbie Lundberg, Paul Michelman, Jinette Ramos, and Lauren Rosano.

From Deloitte, we appreciate all the work of our collaborators. We offer particular thanks to Balaji Bondili, Natasha Buckley, Sue Cantrell, Marissa Copeland, Yen Dang, Steve Hatfield, Diana Kearns-Manolatos, Elisabeth Lee, Katherine Mullis, Nicole Nodi, Saurabh Rijhwani, Brenna Sniderman, and many others.

The University of Massachusetts Lowell contributed resources in support of this effort. UMass Lowell colleagues provided academic insights, guidance, and never-ending collegiality and friendship. Special thanks to Chancellors Jacqueline Moloney and Julie Chen; Dean Sandra Richtermeyer; Professors Stuart Freedman, Elana Feldman, Beth Humberd, and Scott Latham; Graduate Assistant Kunal Gujar; and the students of MGMT.4900 (202/208) Strategic Management in the spring of 2022.

We have interviewed executives and thought leaders across a wide spectrum and have been incredibly fortunate to hear stories from all manner of organizations. Leaders shared their struggles with, and their excitement for, workforce ecosystems. We quoted many of our interviewees in the book and are deeply thankful to them for offering their time and perspectives. Appendix A lists interviewees who participated in this research over the past three years.

Other collaborators offered insightful feedback that helped shape our thinking about workforce ecosystems. We thank them all. We offer specific appreciation to Professors Lynda Gratton, Katherine Kellogg, and Daniel Rock. James Moore, a pioneer in business ecosystem thinking, generously shared his wisdom with us.

Of course, an effort of this type requires attention and sacrifices on many nights, weekends, holidays, and vacations that inevitably impact family and friends. For all the calls and work on deadlines that interrupted otherwise scheduled plans (graduations, weddings, household moves, and so on), and for listening to more about workforce ecosystems than you ever wanted to hear, we sincerely thank our families and friends. We could never have completed this book without your patience, tolerance, love, and good humor. You all know who you are, and we dedicate this book to all of you.

Notes

Introduction

1. For instance, during our interview with Markus Graf, vice president of human resources and global head of talent at Novartis, he mentioned, "We talk right now about 110,000 people at Novartis on our own payroll. But we also specifically look at external workers. We talk roughly about 50,000 people that we capture in our systems, and we see this portion continuing to increase." Markus Graf, interview via Zoom with authors, September 21, 2021.

2. Elizabeth J. Altman, Jeff Schwartz, David Kiron, Robin Jones, and Diana Kearns-Manolatos, "Workforce Ecosystems: A New Strategic Approach to the Future of Work," *MIT Sloan Management Review*, April 13, 2021, https://sloan-review.mit.edu/projects/workforce-ecosystems-a-new-strategic-approach-to-the-future-of-work.

3. Juani Swart, Scott Snell, Shad S. Morris, and Casper Boon, "The Ecosystem of Work and Organization: Theoretical Framework and Future Direction," call for papers for a special issue of *Human Resource Management* (2021), https://onlinelibrary.wiley.com/pb-assets/Ecosystem%20of%20Work%20and%20Organization_CfP_Nov%2022-1576001863373.pdf.

4. Yochai Benkler, *The Wealth of Networks: How Social Production Transforms Markets and Freedom* (New Haven, CT: Yale University Press, 2007), https://doi.org/10.1177/1084713807301373.

5. Naomi Climer, "Automation Can Help Humans Enjoy Happy, Productive Working Lives," *Financial Times*, August 26, 2019, https://www.ft.com/content/264915b8-9f4c-11e9-9c06-a4640c9feebb.

6. For a more detailed academic treatment of the craft approach to organizing work, see Jochem Kroezen, Davide Ravasi, Innan Sasaki, Monika Żebrowska,

and Roy Suddaby, "Configurations of Craft: Alternative Models for Organizing Work," *Academy of Management Annals* 15, no. 2 (July 15, 2021): 502–536, https://doi.org/10.5465/annals.2019.0145.

Chapter 1

1. We recognize that some organizations have started to adopt the phrase *extended workforce* to refer to various combinations of people and organizations contributing to their work. For example, Google uses it this way: "The people we employ directly and our extended workforce of vendors, temporary staff, and independent contractors." "About Google's Extended Workforce," Google, https://about.google/extended-workforce. In contrast, we use the term more broadly as we encompass all actors contributing to an organization's strategic goals. For instance, we include complementors and technologies (e.g., bots). While we recognize there may be some confusion with increased usage, we find the phrase helpful as a way to capture the notion of an expanded group of contributors.

2. "LinkedIn Raises $12.8 Million from Bessemer Venture Partners and European Founders Fund to Accelerate Global Growth," LinkedIn Corporate Communications, Categories: Company News, https://news.linkedin.com/2007/01/linkedin-raises-128-million-from-bessemer-venture-partners-and-european-founders-fund-to-accelerate-global-growth.

3. Doron Reuveni, interview via Zoom with authors, September 29, 2020; "About Us: Quick Stats," uTest, https://www.utest.com/about-us.

4. All references to dollars in this book refer to US dollars.

5. "About," Walmart Corporate, https://corporate.walmart.com/about; "Key Financials (Last Fiscal Year)," *Fortune*, February 2, 2022, https://fortune.com/company/walmart/fortune500.

Chapter 2

1. For excellent examples of early writing about business ecosystems, see James F. Moore, "Predators and Prey: A New Ecology of Competition," *Harvard Business Review* 71, no. 3 (1993): 75–86; Marco Iansiti and Roy Levien, *The Keystone Advantage: What the New Dynamics of Business Ecosystems Mean for Strategy, Innovation, and Sustainability* (Brighton, MA: Harvard Business School Press, 2004).

2. Elizabeth J. Altman and Frank Nagle, "Accelerating Innovation through a Network of Ecosystems: What Companies Can Learn from One of the World's Largest Networks of Accelerator Labs," *MIT Sloan Management Review* 61, no. 4 (Summer 2020): 24–30.

3. Martin Ganco, Rahul Kapoor, and Gwendolyn K. Lee, "From Rugged Landscapes to Rugged Ecosystems: Structure of Interdependencies and Firms' Innovative Search," *Academy of Management Review* 45, no. 3 (July 2020): 646–674; Elizabeth J. Altman, David Kiron, Jeff Schwartz, and Robin Jones, "The Future of Work Is through Workforce Ecosystems," *MIT Sloan Management Review*, January 14, 2021, https://sloanreview.mit.edu/article/the-future-of-work-is-through -workforce-ecosystems.

4. Elizabeth J. Altman, Jeff Schwartz, David Kiron, Robin Jones, and Diana Kearns-Manolatos, "Workforce Ecosystems: A New Strategic Approach to the Future of Work," *MIT Sloan Management Review*, April 13, 2021, https://sloan review.mit.edu/projects/workforce-ecosystems-a-new-strategic-approach-to -the-future-of-work.

5. Peter G. Klein, Joseph T. Mahoney, Anita M. McGahan, and Christos N. Pitelis, "Organizational Governance Adaptation: Who Is In, Who Is Out, and Who Gets What," *Academy of Management Review* 44, no. 1 (January 3, 2019): 6–27, https://doi.org/10.5465/amr.2014.0459.

6. Richard Makadok and Russell Coff, "Both Market and Hierarchy: An Incentive-System Theory of Hybrid Governance Forms," *Academy of Management Review* 34, no. 2 (April 1, 2009): 297–319, https://doi.org/10.5465/amr .2009.36982628.

7. For a thorough and accessible definition of software bots, see "What Are Bots?—Definition and Explanation," Kaspersky, Resource Center, Home Security, https://www.kaspersky.com/resource-center/definitions/what-are-bots.

8. "Mayo Clinic Innovation Exchange: Home Page," Mayo Foundation for Medical Education and Research, https://innovationexchange.mayoclinic.org.

9. David B. Yoffie and Mary Kwak, "With Friends Like These: The Art of Managing Complementors," *Harvard Business Review* 84, no. 9 (September 2006): 88–98, https://hbr.org/2006/09/with-friends-like-these-the-art-of-managing-com plementors.

10. Christoph Bode, Stephan M. Wagner, Kenneth J. Petersen, and Lisa M. Ellram, "Understanding Responses to Supply Chain Disruptions: Insights from

Information Processing and Resource Dependence Perspectives," *Academy of Management Journal* 54, no. 4 (November 30, 2017): 833–856, https://doi.org/10 .5465/amj.2011.64870145.

11. "Polaris Announces Partnership with Zero Motorcycles to Co-Develop Electric Vehicles as a Cornerstone of rEV'd Up—Polaris' New Electrification Strategy," Polaris, September 29, 2020, https://www.polaris.com/en-us/news /company/polaris-announces-zero-motorcycles-partnership.

12. Obi Anyanwu, "Havaianas and Disney Announce New Partnership," Fashion Network, August 11, 2015, https://us.fashionnetwork.com/news/havaianas -and-disney-announce-new-partnership,559199.html.

13. William M. Evan and Paul Olk, "R&D Consortia: A New U.S. Organizational Form," *MIT Sloan Management Review* 31, no. 3 (Spring 1990): 37, https://www.proquest.com/openview/2a91c73ff1bb2cd08783a0c283d83688/1 ?pq-origsite=gscholar&cbl=26142.

Chapter 3

1. Shane Greenstein, Karim Lakhani, and Christian Godwin, "Threadless: The Renewal of an Online Community," Harvard Business School Publishing, no. 9-621-056, February 2021, https://hbsp.harvard.edu/search?N=&Nrpp=25&Ntt =threadless&searchLocation=header.

2. Graham, "LEGO Exclusive: AFOLs Taught Us to Take Adults Seriously," Brick Fanatics, January 7, 2021, https://www.brickfanatics.com/lego-exclusive -afols-taught-us-to-take-adults-seriously/?utm_source=copy&utm_medium =website&utm_campaign=SocialSnap.

3. "MFi Program," Apple Inc., https://mfi.apple.com.

Chapter 4

1. Reed Hastings and Erin Meyer, *No Rules Rules: Netflix and the Culture of Reinvention* (New York: Penguin Press, 2020).

Chapter 5

1. Frederick Winslow Taylor, *The Principles of Scientific Management* (New York: Harper and Brothers, 1911).

2. "How a Talent Marketplace Can Help with Career Development," SAP, https://www.sap.com/insights/what-is-a-talent-marketplace.html.

3. Hise O. Gibson, "Essays on Operations Management: Setting Employees Up for Success" (PhD diss., Harvard Business School, 2015); Hise O. Gibson, "T-Shaped Managers—One Size Does Not Fit All: Exploratory Study from the Military," working paper 22–003, Harvard Business School, Cambridge, MA, July 2021.

4. Elizabeth J. Altman, David Kiron, Robin Jones, and Diana Kearns-Manolatos, "Workforce Ecosystems," Deloitte, April 13, 2021, https://www2.deloitte.com /us/en/insights/focus/technology-and-the-future-of-work/workforce-ecosys tems-practical-guidance-for-leaders.html.

5. Edgar H. Schein, *Organizational Culture and Leadership* (San Francisco: Jossey-Bass, 1985), ix.

6. For a description of PlanOmatic and its organization, see *PlanOmatic Vision*, PlanOmatic, YouTube, August 2, 2021, https://www.youtube.com/watch?v=ZH uj29IdyjM.

Chapter 6

1. "Architecture," Lexico, https://www.lexico.com/en/definition/architecture.

2. This section is adapted from Elizabeth J. Altman, Katherine C. Kellogg, and David Kiron, "Orchestrating Workforce Ecosystems," in *The Power of Ecosystems: Making Sense of the New Reality for Organizations*, curated by Stuart Crainer (Business Ecosystem Alliance, 2022), 8–20, https://business-ecosystem-alliance .org/2021/10/15/orchestrating-workforce-ecosystems.

3. For more information about this system, see SAP Fieldglass, https://www .fieldglass.com.

4. "PayPal Implements Global External Workforce Management," SAP Field-glass, https://web.archive.org/web/20210421174353/https://www.fieldglass.com /resources/case-studies/paypal.

5. "How a Global Organization Proves SAP Fieldglass' Value through Results," SAP Fieldglass, https://www.fieldglass.com/sites/default/files/2018-03/Siemens -proves-value-SAP-Fieldglass-vendor-management-solution-through-results.pdf.

6. Altman, Kellogg, and Kiron, "Orchestrating Workforce Ecosystems.".

7. Elizabeth J. Altman, Frank Nagle, and Michael L. Tushman, "The Translucent Hand of Managed Ecosystems: Engaging Communities for Value Creation and Capture," *Academy of Management Annals* 16, no. 1 (January 26, 2022), https://doi.org/10.5465/annals.2020.0244.

Chapter 7

1. Indranil Roy, Yves Van Durme, and Maren Hauptmann, "From Jobs to Superjobs," Deloitte Insights, April 11, 2019, https://www2.deloitte.com/us/en/insights/focus/human-capital-trends/2019/impact-of-ai-turning-jobs-into-superjobs.html.

2. Heather Bellini and Ryan Nolan, "The Battle for Our Screens, Part 2: The Future of Work," Goldman Sachs podcast, September 22, 2020, https://www.goldmansachs.com/insights/podcasts/episodes/09-22-2020-the-battle-for-our-screens-part-2.html.

3. Thomas W. Malone, "How Human-Computer 'Superminds' Are Redefining the Future of Work," *MIT Sloan Management Review* 59, no. 4 (2018): 34, 41.

4. Josh Bersin, "The Mad Scramble to Lead the Talent Marketplace Market," Published December 13, 2021, https://joshbersin.com/2021/12/the-mad-scramble-to-lead-the-talent-marketplace-market.

5. Erik Brynjolfsson, John J. Horton, Adam Ozimek, Daniel Rock, Garima Sharma, and Hong-Yi TuYe, "COVID-19 and Remote Work: An Early Look at US Data," working paper 27344, National Bureau of Economic Research, June 2020, https://www.nber.org/papers/w27344.

6. Marc Harrison, "What One Health System Learned about Providing Digital Services in the Pandemic," *Harvard Business Review*, December 11, 2020, https://hbr.org/2020/12/what-one-health-system-learned-about-providing-digital-services-in-the-pandemic.

7. Dawn Graham, "A Powerful Resume Lesson from History," *Forbes*, December 11, 2018, https://www.forbes.com/sites/dawngraham/2018/12/11/a-powerful-resume-lesson-from-history/?sh=11ddd7d51035.

8. "About Us," Velocity Career Labs, https://www.velocitycareerlabs.com/about.

9. Jeff Schwartz with Suzanne Riss, *Work Disrupted: Opportunity, Resilience, and Growth in the Accelerated Future of Work* (Hoboken, NJ: John Wiley and Sons, 2021), 29–30.

10. Hemant K. Bhargava, Olivier Rubel, Elizabeth J. Altman, Ramnik Arora, Jörn Boehnke, Kaitlin Daniels, Timothy Derdenger, et al., "Platform Data Strategy," *Marketing Letters* 31, no. 4 (2020): 323–334.

Chapter 8

1. "Decent Work," International Labour Organization, https://www.ilo.org/global/topics/decent-work/lang--en/index.html.

2. "Factoring High-Skills Freelancers into the Enterprise Equation," *Managing the Future of Work*, podcast, Harvard Business School, February 24, 2021, https://www.hbs.edu/managing-the-future-of-work/podcast/Pages/podcast-details.aspx?episode=18068591.

3. Elizabeth J. Altman, Katherine C. Kellogg, and David Kiron, "Orchestrating Workforce Ecosystems," in *The Power of Ecosystems: Making Sense of the New Reality for Organizations*, curated by Stuart Crainer (Business Ecosystem Alliance, 2022), 8–20, https://business-ecosystem-alliance.org/2021/10/15/orchestrating-workforce-ecosystems.

Chapter 9

1. Michael Schrage, David Kiron, Bryan Hancock, and Raffaele Breschi, "Performance Management's Digital Shift," *MIT Sloan Management Review*, February 26, 2019, https://sloanreview.mit.edu/projects/performance-managements-digital-shift.

2. Shane Mcfeely and Ben Wigert, "This Fixable Problem Costs U.S. Businesses $1 Trillion," Gallup, March 13, 2019, https://www.gallup.com/workplace/247391/fixable-problem-costs-businesses-trillion.aspx#:~:text=The%20cost%20of%20replacing%20an,to%20%242.6%20million%20per%20year.

Chapter 10

1. Of course even in this broader context, certain fundamental ethical obligations persist. Companies need to respect human rights, for example, in all contexts. These rights include those covered in the Universal Declaration of Human Rights. See https://www.un.org/en/about-us/universal-declaration-of-human-rights.

2. Richard E. Ocejo, "The Virtue of Opportunity: Moral Framing, Community, and Conditional Gentrification," *Social Problems*, September 19, 2021, spab047, https://doi.org/10.1093/socpro/spab047.

3. "Diversity and Inclusion Workforce Sourcing: Study Reveals 8 Key Takeaways for Improving D&I," *HRO Today Flash Report* 5, no. 6 (2021), https://www.hrotoday.com/market-intelligence/research/diversity-inclusion-workforce-sourcing-8-key-takeaways-for-improving-di; Elizabeth J. Altman, David Kiron, Robin Jones, and Jeff Schwartz, "Orchestrating Workforce Ecosystems: Strategically Managing Work across and beyond Organizational Boundaries," MIT Sloan Management Review and Deloitte, May 2022, https://sloanreview .mit.edu/projects/orchestrating-workforce-ecosystems.

4. Peter Loftus, "Justice Department Sues Regeneron over Payments to Copay-Assistance Charity," *Wall Street Journal*, June 24, 2020, https://www.wsj.com /articles/justice-department-sues-regeneron-over-payments-to-copay-assistance-charity-11593024042.

5. Paul M. Barrett, *Who Moderates the Social Media Giants? A Call to End Outsourcing*, NYU Stern School, June 2020, https://bhr.stern.nyu.edu/tech-content -moderation-june-2020?_ga=2.192995821.114743082.1635285481-813725839 .1634865440.

6. Billy Perrigo, "Inside Facebook's African Sweatshop," *Time*, February 17, 2022, https://time.com/6147458/facebook-africa-content-moderation-employee -treatment.

7. "Improving Safety by Working Together," Shell, https://www.shell.com/sus tainability/safety/our-approach/improving-safety-by-working-together.html.

8. Quoted in "Improving Safety by Working Together."

9. "Safety," Weyerhaeuser, https://www.weyerhaeuser.com/company/values /safety.

10. Some sexual assaults occurred between passengers.

11. Geoffrey Fowler, "Uber CEO Q&A: When Rape Happens in an Uber; Who's Responsible?," *Washington Post*, December 6, 2019, https://www.wash ingtonpost.com/technology/2019/12/06/uber-ceo-qa-when-rape-happens-an -uber-whos-responsible.

12. Lynn Sharp Paine, *Value Shift: Why Companies Must Merge Social and Financial Imperatives to Achieve Superior Performance* (New York: McGraw Hill, 2002).

13. Lauren Weber, "50,000 Jobs, 900,000 Resumes: Coronavirus Is Redeploying Workers at Record Pace," *Wall Street Journal*, April 15, 2020, https://web .archive.org/web/20220119042620/https://www.wsj.com/articles/inside-the -push-to-redeploy-workers-quickly-11586943000.

14. Quoted in Josh Rivera, "Furloughed Hilton Workers Offered Access to Other Jobs during Coronavirus Pandemic," *USA Today*, March 23, 2020, https:// www.usatoday.com/story/money/2020/03/23/hilton-employees-furloughs -coronavirus-covid-19-jobs/2893323001.

15. Rivera, "Furloughed Hilton Workers."

16. Quoted in Joann S. Lublin, "We Have Layoffs. You Need Workers," *Wall Street Journal*, February 22, 2021, R1.

17. "Diversity and Inclusion Workforce Sourcing."

18. Altman et al., "Orchestrating Workforce Ecosystems."

19. Sundiatu Dixon-Fyle, Kevin Dolan, Vivian Hunt, and Sara Prince, "Diversity Wins: How Inclusion Matters," McKinsey and Company, May 19, 2020, https://www.mckinsey.com/featured-insights/diversity-and-inclusion/diversity -wins-how-inclusion-matters.

20. "Diversity: The Foundation of Our Success," Bosch, https://www.bosch.com /stories/diversity-at-bosch.

21. Amartya Sen, *Development as Freedom* (New York: Anchor Books, 1999), 7.

22. Stephen Frost and Raafi-Karim Alidina, *Building an Inclusive Organization: Leveraging the Power of a Diverse Workforce* (London: Kogan Page, 2019), xxiv (emphasis added).

23. "Shell-Contractor Safety Leadership: A Collaborative Journey," Shell, https:// www.shell.com/sustainability/safety/our-approach/_jcr_content/par/textim age.stream/1617866361256/e2ebf763dd998742c3046231014eff85d12a8aeb/shell -contractor-safety-leadership-a-collaborative-journey.pdf.

Chapter 11

1. "The Dunlop Commission on the Future of Worker-Management Relations," final report, Catherwood Library Electronic Archive, https://ecommons.cornell .edu/bitstream/handle/1813/79039/DunlopCommissionFutureWorkerManage mentFinalReport.pdf?sequence=1&isAllowed=y.

2. "The Dunlop Commission on the Future of Worker-Management Relations."

3. David Weil, *The Fissured Workplace: Why Work Became So Bad for So Many and What Can Be Done to Improve It* (Cambridge, MA: Harvard University Press, 2017).

4. Pamela J. Loprest and Demetra Smith Nightingale, "The Nature of Work and the Social Safety Net," Urban Institute, July 23, 2018, https://www.urban.org /research/publication/nature-work-and-social-safety-net.

5. Angela M. Antonelli, Christopher Woika, and Laura Kim, "The Changing Nature of Work: More Can Be Done to Help Contingent Workers Save for Retirement," Center for Retirement Initiatives, Georgetown University, November 2017, https://cri.georgetown.edu/the-changing-nature-of-work-more-can-be -done-to-help-contingent-workers-save-for-retirement/.

6. Arne L. Kalleberg, *Precarious Lives: Job Insecurity and Well-being in Rich Democracies* (Cambridge, UK: Polity Books, 2018).

7. Kalleberg's (*Precarious Lives*, 3) full definition of precarious work is work that is *"uncertain, unstable,* and *insecure* and in which employees bear the risks of work (as opposed to business or the government) and *receive limited social benefits and statutory entitlements."*

8. Antonelli, Woika, and Kim, "The Changing Nature of Work."

9. Justin Schweitzer and Rose Khattar, "It's a Good Jobs Shortage: The Real Reason So Many Workers Are Quitting," Center for American Progress, December 07, 2021, https://www.americanprogress.org/article/its-a-good-jobs-shortage -the-real-reason-so-many-workers-are-quitting.

10. "Decent Work," International Labour Organization, https://www.ilo.org /global/topics/decent-work/lang--en/index.html.

11. Directorate-General for Internal Policies Committee on Employment and Social Affairs, "The Lisbon Strategy," European Parliament, 2009–2014, https:// bit.ly/3stvjIo.

12. Jeff Schwartz with Suzanne Riss, *Work Disrupted: Opportunity, Resilience, and Growth in the Accelerated Future of Work* (Hoboken, NJ: John Wiley and Sons, 2021), 29–30.

13. Courtney Connley, "Work Amazon, Facebook and 8 Other Companies That Have Committed to Raising Their Minimum Wage," CNBC, May 25, 2019,

https://www.cnbc.com/2019/05/24/glassdoor-10-companies-that-have-com mitted-to-raising-minimum-wage.html.

14. Agnieszka Piasna, "Where Do We Stand with 'More and Better' Jobs in Europe?," Social Europe, January 24, 2018, https://socialeurope.eu/where-do -we-stand-with-more-and-better-jobs-in-europe.

15. Tanya Goldman and David Weil, "Who's Responsible Here? Establishing Legal Responsibility in the Fissured Workplace," working paper no. 114, Institute for New Economic Thinking, February 18, 2020, https://www.ineteconom ics.org/uploads/papers/WP_114-Goldman-Weil.pdf.

16. "What Is Economic Security?," International Committee of the Red Cross, June 18, 2015, https://www.icrc.org/en/document/introduction-economic -security.

17. Jonathan P. Hiatt, "Policy Issues concerning the Contingent Work Force," *Washington and Lee Law Review* 52, no. 739 (June 1, 1995), https://scholarly commons.law.wlu.edu/wlulr/vol52/iss3/5.

18. Steven Greenhouse, "In Biggest Drive since 1937, Union Gains a Victory," *New York Times*, February 26, 1999, https://www.nytimes.com/1999/02/26/us /in-biggest-drive-since-1937-union-gains-a-victory.html.

19. "The Dunlop Commission on the Future of Worker-Management Relations."

20. Ronald W. Schatz, *The Labor Board Crew: Remaking Worker-Employer Relations from Pearl Harbor to the Reagan Era* (Champaign: University of Illinois Press, January 11, 2021).

21. Edward Carlier, Eric van Dam, and Ben Smith, "EU Proposes New Legislation to Protect 'Digital Labor Platform' Workers from Status Misclassification," JD Supra, December 15, 2021, https://www.jdsupra.com/legalnews/eu -proposes-new-legislation-to-protect-1848075.

22. It is estimated that twenty-eight million people in the European Union work on or through digital labor platforms. By 2025, that number is expected to rise to forty-three million, about 10 percent of the entire EU population (in 2021). See Carlier, van Dam, and Smith, "EU Proposes New Legislation"; "Population and Population Change Statistics," Eurostat Statistics Explained, July 5, 2021, https://ec.europa.eu/eurostat/statistics-explained/index.php?title=Population _and_population_change_statistics#:~:text=On%201%20January%202021,%20 the,less%20than%20the%20previous%20year.

23. Carlier, van Dam, and Smith, "EU Proposes New Legislation."

24. Alli Brace, "Pay Parity Laws Encourage Companies to Realign Their Work-force," VNDLY, September 16, 2021, https://www.vndly.com/pay-parity-laws -encourage-companies-to-realign-their-workforce-blg21.

25. Daisuke Wakabayashi, "Google Could Be Violating Labor Laws with Pay for Temp Workers," *New York Times*, September 10, 2021, https://www.nytimes. com/2021/09/10/technology/google-temporary-workers-labor-laws-pay.html.

26. Elizabeth J. Altman, Jeff Schwartz, David Kiron, Robin Jones, and Diana Kearns-Manolatos, "Workforce Ecosystems: A New Strategic Approach to the Future of Work," *MIT Sloan Management Review*, April 13, 2021, https://sloan review.mit.edu/projects/workforce-ecosystems-a-new-strategic-approach-to -the-future-of-work.

27. Lynda Gratton and Andrew J. Scott, *The 100-Year Life: Living and Working in an Age of Longevity* (London: Bloomsbury Publishing, December 28, 2021); Steven Johnson, *Extra Life: A Short History of Living Longer* (New York: Riverhead Books, May 11, 2021).

28. Josh Bersin, "Why Udemy Could Be the Hottest Company in Corporate Learning," December 9, 2021, https://joshbersin.com/2021/11/why-udemy -could-be-the-hottest-company-in-corporate-learning/.

29. Kalleberg, *Precarious Lives*, 4.

Chapter 12

1. David Weil, *The Fissured Workplace: Why Work Became So Bad for So Many and What Can Be Done to Improve It* (Cambridge, MA: Harvard University Press, 2017).

2. Statista Research Department, "The Staffing Industry Worldwide—Statistics and Facts," Statista, February 7, 2022, https://www.statista.com/topics/5689 /the-staffing-industry-worldwide/#topicHeader__wrapper.

3. Erik van Vulpen, "Revenue per Employee: Definition, Formula, and Calcu-lation," AIHR: Academy to Innovate HR, https://www.aihr.com/blog/revenue -per-employee.

4. Agnieszka Piasna, "Where Do We Stand with 'More and Better' Jobs in Europe?," Social Europe, January 24, 2018, https://socialeurope.eu/where-do -we-stand-with-more-and-better-jobs-in-europe.

5. "Job Quality," Organisation for Economic Co-operation and Development, https://www.oecd.org/statistics/job-quality.htm; "Lumina Foundation, Gates Foundation and Omidyar Network Tell Full Story of U.S. Job Quality," Gallup, https://www.gallup.com/analytics/318188/great-jobs-success-story.aspx; "Good Jobs Project," Center on Education and the Workforce, Georgetown University, https://cew.georgetown.edu/good-jobs-project.

6. Weil, *The Fissured Workplace*.

Index